Urban Gothic

Tales of Debauchery, Pillage, and Other Strange Events

By Jason Goodman

Other Books by the Author:

BLOOD ON MY HANDS and a knife in my back
SIMPLE REFLECTIONS on a frozen surface
NERVOUS READER
NERVOUS READER second edition
a. PUZZLED EXISTENCE

Available at Amazon.com or wherever fine books are sold.

DISCLAIMER

During the research and writing of this book, every attempt was made to disguise the identities of the individuals portrayed. Names have been changed. Time periods and exact locations have been altered whenever reference is made to a particular individual or event.

However, the author wants to clarify that every

story in this book is based on facts, diverging from the absolute truth only in the circumstances described above. The author considers the identity of the characters depicted in these stories to be "Everyman." Thus, *Urban Gothic* stands as a metaphor for the trials and tribulations of all of humanity.

Inquiries:

Alchemy Studio, Inc. Art & Design –
Fine literary works
Lititz, Pennsylvania, and Westport, Ireland
www.alchemystudioinc.com

Front-cover design and back-cover photograph by:
Jason P. Goodman

Cover Design:
Joshua Riggan

Copy Editing/Proofreading:
Frank W. Kresen
www.artisanproofpositive.com

artisan :: **proof positive**
professional graphic design and editorial services

Interior Layout Design:
Kimberly A. Walsh
www.artisankimwalsh.com

Printed in the United States of America
ISBN#: 978-0-578-14350-7
Library of Congress Control Number: 2017900181

Table of Contents

The Stories

A Few ACTUAL Ghost Stories

Dedication

*A*ll of the characters portrayed in this volume of stories have made it possible for me to write it. I would like to thank them for providing me with the zest of a colorful life. We must never lose sight of the humor surrounding us. Even in pathos, one can find some humor. It is simply a matter of observation.

All of life is a stage, and we are but comedians upon that platform, transforming a serious entity called "life" into something that is absurd, laughable, and palatable.

*I*n memory of my brother Bill, a great man who died too young. He loved to laugh, mostly at life's absurdity, and I made him laugh just hours before his death.

I miss you, Bill.

I have an immense sweet tooth, and I go through various periods of desserts. At one time, I made Carrot Cake my dessert of choice. My brother Bill, who fought and overcame his own demons concerning weight, left this image on my door one day. It was his way of reminding me that whatever went "in" would stay there. I was "The Carrot Cake Kid"!

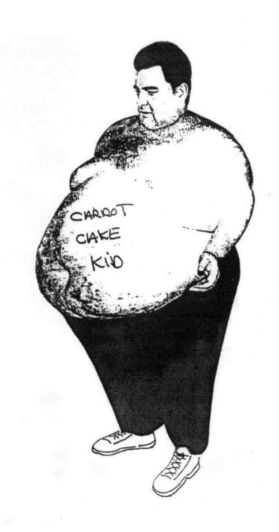

Preface

*M*ost of my life, I have been fascinated by ghost stories and dark, foreboding castles with bats flying about and sinister specters in every window. My library is packed with books from the four corners of the earth detailing what many profess to be true and accurate stories of paranormal activity. It seems that every country has its own ghost tales to tell.

Allow me to inform you right now that this particular volume is not one of those tomes.

"Urban" pertains to a city or town. When applied to a person, it means someone who is "citified." "Gothic," on the other hand, outside all of the references to architecture and those pesky Goths, who were the scourge of the Roman Empire, is a genre of literature beset with gloomy, mysterious, or even sinister settings.

Then, there's the use of "Gothic" that refers to a certain sans-serif (no frills or heads and tails to the letters) typeface that uses a square-cut form.

What has all of this got to do with the contents of this book? Granted, there are a few real ghost stories being told here (see pages 339-357). These things actually happened. I have been very careful to relate these tales in a most concise yet complete manner. Being someone born under the star sign of Aquarius, I am not prone to anything fanatical or of a fanciful nature. I have always found myself seeking the truth behind any seemingly odd occurrence. This is what makes these few real ghost stories so poignant. They actually happened, and, to this day, I cannot offer a logical explanation for why or how they occurred.

But these are relatively few in number compared to the bulk of the stories in this collection. I have derived a majority of the material from life, whether from an employment-related situation or humorous events that happen daily. Every one of these is a small vignette plucked from time and space and given life on the written page. I have used the term "Urban Gothic" to describe events whose origin can be found in the pathos of living.

Consider this: I was born in Wilkes-Barre, Pennsylvania. This was a terrible place to grow up. It was a coal town — dirty, grey, and miserable. Everything was the color of the slate that coal miners pulled from the earth. The entire area had the same hue — grey and dismal.

In Wilkes-Barre, there were the rich mine operators, and then there was everyone else — the poor people who dug that black scourge out of the ground. My father was a coal miner when I was born, and our family was poor. Our house didn't have many nice things hanging on its walls, but I do remember one item in particular. It was a cast-iron trivet, one of those things you use under hot cookware. It hung from the wall with a little piece of red Christmas ribbon. That trivet hung there on a nail — always in the same place — for my entire life. It never moved until the house and my parents' lives took on an estate executor. On that little cast-iron thing were these words: *Laughter Is the Best Medicine.*

Hopefully, that is what I may bring to you today — some laughter.

Help me explore the parts of life that need to be shared. Every story in this collection is true, and I have taken great pains in retelling them. Each is a true and actual event retold as accurately as my memory and research can provide.

Please, rest assured: I have paid a handsome deductible on these premium adventures. Age and acquired wisdom have not been kind to any new generation of stories in this genre. I have slowed down in my writing endeavors to the point of mediocrity. But before I lose the edge permanently, I have managed to put into words the tales contained in this collection, *Urban Gothic*.

I sincerely hope that you enjoy the effort.

Introduction

*I*f you look up the word *"authentic"* in *Webster's Dictionary,* you will see a photo of Jason Goodman.

Actually, I just made that up. But it *is* how I feel.

I have never met Jason face to face. But I feel that we went to different schools together. He's the kind of guy most guys would kill to be — including me. A down-to-earth Jack-of-All Trades, mechanically hyper-savvy, streetwise Easterner who excels at the fine arts and who can quote Greek and Roman classics of literature.

Jason claims that every story in *Urban Gothic* is an actual episode — one that really occurred — from his life. There is no fiction in this book. The stories are all slices of his life — snapshots frozen in time. He admits and stresses that his childhood was in — and of — another time: an America that no longer is, an America that, if it were a TV show, would be in black-and-white, not color.

There is no distinction between his life and the

things he writes about. The fact that some stories in *Urban Gothic* border on the unbelievable, on the comically absurd, does not change the fact that they all actually happened. Think *Holden Caulfield Grows Up, Discovers LSD, and Turns into a self-published — but Just as Gonzo — Hunter Thompson.*

Jason appears to have done nothing in his life half-heartedly. When he's in, he's all in.

From growing up in a tiny coal town in Pennsylvania — and escaping the cycle of poverty that would have killed a lesser man — to a combat role in Vietnam, to PTSD and overcoming a monster alcohol addiction, to his fascination with American muscle cars and foreign sports cars, to his mastery of heavy-duty construction machinery, to two divorces and a lasting third marriage to his beloved Teresa, to pursuing academic degrees that led him into teaching art to prison convicts in America and to high-schoolers in Australia, to pursuing the fine arts and becoming an accomplished, world-class painter, to traveling the USA and becoming a savvy citizen of the world, Jason seems to have done it all. He has lived more in his lifetime than most people could even dream of, even if they were given the gift of limitless reincarnation.

— Frank W. Kresen, ed.

The Stories

Death of a Coiffure

*O*utside of the city of Nanticoke, Pennsylvania, there is a small suburb called Honey Pot. This little community is nestled in the slag heaps, and there is only one road in and one road out.

It was 1968, and I was driving a 1956 Thunderbird and wearing a double-breasted light-blue blazer with an ascot and matching breast-pocket handkerchief. You could say that I was an up-and-coming, studly type of guy. Back then, in a time that now seems like someone else's life, I met this girl who happened to reside, with her Polish-speaking parents, in Honey Pot, Pennsylvania. So I invited her out to dinner.

On that fateful night, I drove down there, and, of course, she wasn't ready, but she said that I should sit and watch television, because it was "...*in color*...." You see, that was a big deal back then. To have a full-color television was something special. Prior to this, if you weren't able to afford one of these technological wonders, you could buy pieces of colored plastic, which you could stick onto the screen, imparting an amber, if not orange, coloration to the black-and-white picture.

I didn't have the heart to tell her that we had at least four of these color televisions at our house. The reason for this can be found in my first book, *a. Puzzled Existence,* if you are interested. I remember that it was cold, a typical Pennsylvania winter night in this coal region. For Christmas the year previous, my mother gave all of us boys brand-new butane cigarette lighters — even though none of us smoked.

That, obviously, didn't matter. She said that every "gentleman" should have the means to light a lady's cigarette, and that was important.

Please understand: This was no "small stocking stuffer." A gold "Swank" butane cigarette lighter was no inexpensive proposition. So, on this night, I had my "gentleman's" compulsory cigarette lighter on my person.

When my date emerged from the back room, I was aghast. She was wearing a shocking-pink dress with silver-sequined shoes. But, more importantly, her hair matched her shoes — it was silver, and it was piled high on her head in the fashion of Marge Simpson, from today's TV animated sitcom *The Simpsons.*

Our destination was the famous "Iorio's" restaurant, located on Route 115, a few miles outside of Wilkes-Barre. The place was nice. It was the restaurant of choice for the local Mafia chieftains and a favorite with the young men of the area for a "leg opener" first date. The "Florence Gardens Hotel" was only a few miles up the mountain (if you catch my drift).

Iorio's had a somewhat romantic atmosphere: Candles on every table, low, mood lighting and a gentleman dressed in a white shirt, black bow tie, and red vest, walking around playing beautiful strains on his shiny violin. It was the perfect atmosphere for small talk and long, drawn-out summaries of one's achievements designed to impress the opposite sex with one's manliness.

I was in fine form that evening, piling on the small table a series of reasons why this woman should ask me to ravage her later. I would return home with that knowing smile of contentedness.

Finally, after an appetizer and main course, she reached into her little silver handbag and lifted out a pack of "Virginia Slims." Naturally, she didn't have a pack of matches, so I rose to the occasion and withdrew my brand-new "Swank" gold-plated butane-powered cigarette lighter. With measured movements, I leaned across the table and looked into her well-made-up eyes. In 1968, black eyeliner was a prominent fashion statement in Honey Pot. Everything seemed to glow in a rose-colored mist — the candlelight, the violin playing in the background, the aroma of good Italian food in the air.

I carefully flicked open the lighter and pushed the gold-plated toggle. What happened next is the stuff of nightmares.

Much to my surprise, a huge flame, about two feet long, shot from my Swank gold-plated cigarette lighter, but even that wasn't the worst issue. Much to my chagrin, the flame reduced her pile of highly teased and hair-sprayed coiffure to a smoldering heap. Her eyebrows simply disappeared under the onslaught of my gold-plated blowtorch. The room was momentarily aglow with the light from the blaze, and the violin player scratched the bow across the strings in a horrible sound reminiscent of the infamous shower scene in Alfred Hitchcock's *Psycho*.

The place grew absolutely silent. Time seemed to stop completely in those few seconds, and I envisioned myself being incarcerated for the remainder of my life, chained in some subterranean dungeon and suffering unspeakable tortures.

Well, thankfully, that didn't happen. What did

happen was that a lot of my father's money changed hands — exactly how much, I was never told. But it must have been a considerable amount, based on my father's reactions for the next four years whenever the incident would come up.

As for me, needless to say, the young lady never returned my phone calls. I can't say I blamed her, as my own actions immediately following the incident were less than honorable. I left her some money for a cab to take her home, jumped in my souped-up Thunderbird, and sped away into the night.

How was I to know there was a flame control on my "Swank" gold-plated butane cigarette lighter?

Sushi in Key West

*T*here were two excavating companies in Key West, and I worked for both of them. I operated heavy equipment for one of them, Clarence Keevan & Son.

The "son" in "Clarence Keevan & Son" was an interesting story, actually a bit tragic. He was standing on top of a drum trailer directing a loader operator when lightning struck — literally. His arm was extended, and he had one foot on the truck body. The lightning passed through his body, welding together the links of the gold chain that was around his neck and burning him something awful. The bolt exited out his left leg into the truck frame. I guess it was touch and go for a while afterwards, but he did recover. Well, not completely, but the man was alive — let's put it that way.

Another interesting little tidbit having to do with this company was the story about the mechanic. Back in the 1950s, this guy had been the first Russian to defect to the West in a MIG fighter jet. The man worked on these planes and told me that he had to go up in them with the pilot, who wore a parachute. The mechanic did not. Thus, if anything happened, the mechanic was expected to go down with the ship. Nice warranty on that buggy.

Anyway, it was something right out of James Bond. The mechanic managed to sneak into a plane and take off. The USSR scrambled planes to shoot him down, and the US scrambled planes to keep him alive. He said that the USSR's planes were really close when he crossed over into West German airspace.

I asked how he knew how to fly the thing, and he told me that he didn't. He just watched the pilots and did what he'd seen them do. The problem was with landing. When he came in, he didn't know how to stop the thing. So the plane just rolled and bumped into a building at the very end of the runway.

Our guys questioned him for a few days, and, when he went back to the airport, his entire jet fighter had been dismantled and packed away in shipping crates. The US government gave the mechanic citizenship, $100,000, and a change of identity because the KGB would have killed him if they knew where he lived.

Through a series of marriages and missteps, he wound up working as a heavy-equipment mechanic in Key West, Florida — a place that seems to attract people with really unusual life stories.

So, I was working with two other guys and one Cuban laborer. We built roads and parking lots all over the NAS (Naval Air Station) on Stock Island. In the meantime, my wife was working at the Half Shell Raw Bar in Margaritaville. It was the busiest restaurant in Key West. Well, look at it this way: I worked seven days a week, 6:00 a.m. to 6:00 p.m. every day — 84 hours a week. One day I was looking at my paycheck. After taxes and all of the other deductions, my pay came to $660. You have to keep in mind that half of your pay in Florida — a "right to work" state — was the sunshine. Teresa, my wife, had made almost $600 the night before in a matter of six hours — in cash, from tips alone. What is wrong with this picture?

The powers-that-be at the Raw Bar decided that they would offer sushi. They flew in a chef from Japan and set up the entire operation. Late at night, the chef would give away the sashimi and sushi that had not been sold. He actually had to sell it or toss it out — it was the law. Teresa would bring home all of this marvelous sushi, and I started taking it to work for my lunch.

One day we started preparing for lunch, with the four of us sitting under a palm tree. I opened my lunch bag and pulled this stuff out. Then I made the mistake of asking my co-workers if they wanted any. The one real redneck in our crew looked over in disgust and said, "Hell, man — you're eatin' bait! That's the stuff I use for bait."

They all packed up their thermos bottles and lunch boxes and moved to another palm tree. I usually ate my lunch alone after that.

Back to my job with Keevan & Son Excavating. I would get up at 5:00 a.m. and grab a cup of coffee and my lunch. Then I'd roar down US 1 to the Naval Base. At the gate, they would always stop me, even though I had a full security clearance. It was my truck that bothered them. I'd bought a 1958 Chevy truck from the Half Shell Raw Bar. It ran like a top, but it was all rusted out. One day, while flying down the road, late for work, as usual, the roof just ripped right off and blew into a mangrove swamp. After that, I had a convertible truck that I named "Bad Dog." The sentries didn't find any of this amusing and made my life difficult. "Hell," I tried to tell them, "this is art," but to no avail.

At about 10 minutes to 6:00 a.m., I would start

my machine, a Ford backhoe, after I'd checked all of the fluids and shot some grease into the business end of the machine. I usually couldn't wait to start the thing, because the mosquitoes were totally out of control, and the diesel fumes would chase most of them away. At 6:00 a.m., during the summer, the temperature was already over 90 degrees; worse yet was the humidity — it would be 95%.

I'd proceed to operate this really hot machine all day in that sun. My uniform (yes, we had uniforms) would be soaking wet all day long, and anywhere there was shade, there were those mosquitoes, just waiting to attack.

One day, my Cuban laborer and I were driving to another job; he was sitting on the fender. As we rounded a curve, there on the road in front of us were two sailors, holding a huge jet engine, trying to keep it from rolling into a swamp. So, we stopped and helped these poor guys out and saved the American taxpayers a few million dollars.

I mean, it begged to be asked: What, exactly, were these two boys doing out in the middle of nowhere on the Naval Air Station with a large jet engine? But they just thanked us profusely, and we went our separate ways.

Little did I know then that that little act of

kindness would prevent my being placed in front of a firing squad later on.

All day long, the Fl4s would be doing "touch and go's" on the main runway, and, naturally, that was exactly where I had to work. When those bastards would hit that after-burner, I could feel my insides slapping against my skin. This would go on for 12 hours some days. One day, I was operating a grader — one of those big, long machines with the blade in the center, mounted up underneath the frame. My boss man told me to pack it up and clean everything off of my machine because we were going to cross the main runway. Yep — we were crossing when the Fl4s were doing their "touch and go's." So I went to a hose and scrubbed that thing down like it was Saturday-date-night at the drive-in movies.

When it came my turn to run across the runway, a jet just blasted through. My boss waved to me frantically; I gunned the engine and popped the clutch. When I hit the edge of the pavement, a ton of little round rocks few out from underneath my machine and proceeded to cover the entire runway. The Navy has a term for that: "FOS" — something about "foreign objects, blah, blah…"

Well, they went absolutely bizarro-world on me. The pack of angry jet fighters could not land. Those little rocks would have shredded their engines and tires. Next thing I knew, there were a ton of Navy personnel with brooms and shovels — plus a pile of the meanest-looking uniformed officers I'd ever seen.

Needless to say, I got called on the carpet. A firing squad had been assembled, and when they got to the "Any last words?" bit, I mentioned the jet engine that I'd saved from the swamp. "Hold your fire, men. We have to examine this in depth."

In the end, I kept my job and my life. You might debate that I was really "living." It seemed like I was actually in hell, doing a long stretch for a sin I hadn't committed.

Sure, pal: They all say that down here.

Then they say that they are going to write a book and finally end up finding Jesus.

I'll be damned if it ain't true.

Intelligent Deck Apes

I served aboard an LST with the Riverine Force when I was in Vietnam. My rating at that time was Boatswain's Mate, and my rank was "Leading Seaman," which meant that the entire stern division, consisting of 12 men, was under my charge.

One day we were doing what deck apes do, banging on the metal deck with hammers and other chipping devices. We also had an electric deck grinder, which resembled a small wolverine with a mouth full of toothy wheels.

So there we were, beating on this old bucket in 95-degree heat, with a humidity level of the same persuasion. It was bad. Sweat just rolled off of you, and they ordered us to eat salt tablets all day, for fear we would just collapse where we stood.

While in Saigon, many guys would purchase all forms of items, some to be sent home — to "The World," as we called all parts of the planet

that were not in Vietnam. Other items were for
their own enjoyment. These, of course, included
copious amounts of marijuana that was packaged
in a cigarette pack, complete with filters. Even
the cellophane seal was intact. The Vietnamese
sellers would steam open the bottom of the
package, remove the 20 cigarettes, and roll the
tobacco out, which, to them was more important
and valuable than any form of pot. Then, they
would refill each cigarette with clean, seedless
pot. Pretty nifty.

But I'm not here to talk about the various ways
nefarious smoking products are packaged, so I'll
get on with this story.

As we worked in the heat and humidity, I
remembered that one of my guys had purchased
a cassette deck system with two huge speakers.

I asked him if he had any blank cassette tapes,
and he answered in the affirmative. He came up
with a 90-minute tape. Now, please understand
that we were positioned in the stern of the boat,
and our living quarters were located right below
where we worked. There was a ladder and a
hatch that opened up to this area directly from
our area. Also, there was a canvas roof over the
entire area, which meant that you couldn't see
what was happening back there from the bridge.

We set up the cassette deck and speakers and proceeded to make a 90-minute tape of the sounds of our work. Banging, chipping, growling, and, of course, cursing as only sailors know how to do effectively. Then, we started to play the tape back. After that, the most strenuous exercise that took place was getting up to turn the tape over.

So, there we were — 13 men lying around. Some were reading books. Others were sleeping. A few were working on their tans. It was all pleasant in our little paradise until a particular Lieutenant JG (Junior Grade) came waltzing around the corner and stepped into our little candy store.

Just think: 13 sailors, lying around, getting paid the exorbitant fee of just about $90/month while a Japanese cassette player did their work for them.

This guy absolutely turned colors. His face went from Caucasian to red, and then on to purple in a matter of seconds. He was so flustered that he couldn't even speak. The guy just muttered a few phrases and then turned and walked away.

Trust me: I knew this wasn't the end to this little caper. This guy hated my guts because I was a wise-ass, and he didn't like that one bit. He wrote me up, and I had to "stand at Captain's

Mast." This is really serious stuff. If found guilty, I could face confinement and being busted down to a bug under a rock, losing all of that money every month, with no chance of advancement for my entire lifetime.

This Leuy JG came to the "hearing" well prepared. He had a yellow legal pad. It makes one wonder where this guy got a standard yellow legal pad in Vietnam during the middle of a war, anyway. He had pages of notes describing this dreadful scene: All 13 men in position of complete repose, doing absolutely nothing to advance American interests in South Vietnam.

Finally, he produced the errant cassette tape and proceeded to play excerpts of a beautiful racket: 13 hammers and other devices of rust destruction banging away. It sounded like something by Debussy, it was so wonderful.

Meanwhile, the skipper, who was turning red and holding his sides so that he wouldn't burst out laughing, told the man to stop the tape player and interrupted his volley of accusations against me. The Captain, between chuckles, told me never to do that again. He also informed me that he was going to confiscate this cassette tape as evidence and place it under lock and key for eternity as collateral that I would never again perpetrate this activity. I was not to receive any lashes, nor was I going to be keel hauled (these were just a few of the fears that I'd secretly harbored leading up to my trial).

And I became a free man — or sailor, depending upon how you look at it.

I can assure you that I made an enemy for life. This would all come back at me at a future date, while I was anchored in Pearl Harbor.

But that, my friends, is another story.

The Infamous Box Lunch

I spent a season working in the carnival business.

A friend of mine bought a game called "Shooting Waters" and asked me to join him as a barker in this enterprise. The "barker" is the person with the tinny-sounding microphone who is supposed to convince you to part with your hard-earned money, all for a chance to win a cheap little stuffed animal. These types of "prizes" were called "Rats" in the business.

We had an old bread truck that we pulled this game with. It resembled a small mobile home and consisted of a counter with 14 45-caliber pistols that shot out a steady and powerful stream of water. The object of the game was to pop a ping-pong ball out of a clear plastic tube before anyone else. I know — it sounds pretty stupid when it's presented in that fashion, but, trust me: This thing was wildly popular. We spent our evenings counting quarters to the tune of between $1200 and $1500 per night.

Needless to say, I made a lot of money. Plus, I had practically no expenses, because that was part of the deal: Room and board was included. It consisted of a bunk bed in the back of the truck and a gas stove that heated gruel when my friend decided to cook. What I did with some of that loot was plan for a trip in the fall to the West Coast in a sports car. I bought an old "basket case" MGB and proceeded to rebuild it. (For you non-gearheads out there, a "Basket Case" is a vehicle that comes to you in a bunch of bushel baskets. It is like a puzzle that you have to assemble, and a lot of pieces are missing.)

On my days off the road, I worked feverishly on this car. I rebuilt the thing from the ground up, and it came out well. This little MGB was sweet — powder blue with dark-blue leather interior. It had a new engine, a new transmission, and just about everything else that could be removed from under its hood (or *bonnet*, as the British would say). A fresh paint job followed, and then the installation of a radio and an 8-Track tape player.

I was *stylin'*.

Before I left for the coast, I spent a month or two hanging out in Wilkes-Barre, Pennsylvania, just putting the finishing touches on my "B" car.

During that time, I was dating different women, and one day at the local art-association meeting, I met this girl named Andrea. She was attracted to artists, and I just happened to be one. Hell, I would have been a stockbroker if that was the type she was attracted to.

We made plans to travel down to a little town called New Hope. This was a small artists' colony in Pennsylvania that was located along one of the old canals that were built long ago. Now the place is simply a tourist trap with a fancy ice-cream store, where people with screaming kids wait for hours in line just to sample the goodies.

On the way down the turnpike, Andrea told me that I would have to call and tell her mother that we broke down if we were to *"...spend the night together..."* as Mick Jagger once sang about so eloquently. Naturally, I became deeply offended and shouted that I would never say that my MGB — a classic among sports cars — had broken down. Especially after all of the months I had invested in its complete overhaul.

The MGB — and Jaguar, for that matter — used a carburetor of English design called an "SU." Later, the Japanese bought the patent for this piece of equipment and placed them in their Datsun Z cars. These were supposedly designed for racing and, occasionally, would spew out some gasoline when they burped. But there was a special pipe for this that directed the fuel out onto the ground. The leather interior of the car and the faint hint of gasoline combined to give English sports cars their famous smell. It was comfortable — mechanical biceps with notes of gasoline. It smelled like performance.

As we drove down the turnpike, I noticed this terrible odor in my coveted MGB. It smelled bad — not the pleasant combination of gasoline and leather described above. This was just gross. I started to suspect that one of my brothers may have rubbed cheese on my manifold — just as a prank. My brothers did things like that all the time. Some of our pranks on each other were very well designed and almost devious in nature.

Then I thought, *No — out of respect, they wouldn't do that.* I concluded that some animal had climbed up under the hood and had gotten cooked on my exhaust pipe. Finally I asked my date, Andrea, if she smelled anything.

Andrea became animated. She said, "Oh, my — I almost forgot. I brought a little box lunch for us to enjoy on our trip." She proceeded to reach behind the seats and retrieve a shoebox. When she opened it, the entire car filled with this same stench.

I said, "Good God! What in the hell is that?"

She started to pull a ring of very warm *kielbasa* from the box, along with five slices of white bread — the kind you could get for nine cents for a two-foot loaf — and a medium-sized onion.

That was it. No mustard. No napkins. There wasn't even a knife to cut this foul-smelling stuff with.

So, I asked to see the box and its contents. Then, I carefully rolled down the window and threw it out onto the roadway.

If a state trooper had stopped me for littering, I am convinced he'd have let me go after I related this story to him.

That Pesky Closet Skeleton

*F*our out of the eight back surgeries that I've had were performed at the CMC Hospital in Scranton, Pennsylvania. For a while, I was seeing a neurosurgeon there; you might say that we established a relationship with each other over a period of a few years.

CMC Hospital was located on "The Hill" in Scranton, not far from The University of Scranton. It was an eight-story affair, stuck right on the top of the hill that gave this neighborhood its name. Usually, all of the back-surgery patients would be housed on the eighth floor, right under the heliport. CMC was the premier trauma hospital for the entire region, and it was busy on the weekends, with choppers landing every half-hour or so.

I think that it was surgery number four when this event occurred. After a long, drawn-out procedure, I would be transported to the eighth floor to begin my recuperation. After lower-back surgery, they want you to get out of bed and walk. The corridor went entirely around the eighth floor, and that is what I would do — take slow, steady laps around this walkway, popping into my room occasionally to catch my breath.

One day, I was going about the business of recuperation, and I spied an open closet. It contained one of those medical skeletons used for training. It came with its own four-wheel base and was about five feet tall. So I threw a sheet over the thing and rolled it into my room. When I got there, I lifted it off its base and placed it in my bed, with the sheet and covers drawn up. I put the nurse call button in its bony little hand, pushed the button, and ran and hid in the bathroom. After a few minutes, the nurses came storming in and screamed bloody murder. Naturally, they told my doctor.

Later that evening, when the doctor showed up, he came into my room and said, "Jason, what the hell are you doing to my nurses?" So, I told him how that little stunt was a protest directed at the amount of time that would pass from when I would call for a shot of pain medication and the time it arrived.

If he was amused, it didn't show on his face at all.

A Few Feathers

I spent a few years in Boulder, Colorado. It was probably one of the best times of my life, working at a small excavating company, being paid union scale to drive (or rubber) backhoes up to the tree line to work for a few hours.

It was great. I had a British sports car and an apartment on "The Hill" in Boulder. This was, by far, the best address in town because that is where Colorado University is located — and, as Elvis Presley once sang, "...*girls, girls, girls...*"

There were five students sharing the house above me. My place was a daylight basement flat with off-street parking, perfect for a bachelor with a British sports car.

Back in the day (*You know something? I really dislike that expression. Don't ask me why. It's just that there is something just downright wrong about it.*), there was a well-known author, who lectured at UCLA, named Carlos Castaneda. One of his famous books was *The Teachings of Don Juan, a*

Yaqui Priest. Castaneda went down to the wilds of New Mexico and studied the Yaqui Indians and all of their rituals — sweat lodges, mescaline, more sweat lodges, and a lot more mescaline.

In his second book, ol' Carlos talked about the use of peyote, with an emphasis on how to use this compound effectively. One of the main things that you must remember is to never — and I repeat, *never* — drink anything after you have ingested peyote. The urge to do so will be colossal, because peyote tastes like dog turds. It really does. This is the most foul-tasting stuff you will ever place in your mouth — assuming, of course, you would even want to put this into your gob.

Well, the six of us went in on six buttons of peyote. The guy who delivered the stuff was an honest-to-goodness American Indian who lived on a reservation. He told us that he'd harvested this peyote that morning, and I believed him because it was soft and green, really fresh stuff. Russell and I just braved the destruction of our taste buds and popped these "buttons" into our mouths and chomped them up. It was disgusting, to say the least.

Meanwhile, our friends put them into a blender with a bunch of New Age fruit — smoothies, which had just entered the mainstream at this time. They ground it all up and drank it instead of chewing it. The taste was so bad that they had to drink a few beers afterward. As bad as it was, my friend Russell wanted to drink beer — the very thing that Mr. Castaneda had warned us not to do. I had to strong-arm him at one point to prevent this from happening, and it was a good thing. Our partners in crime (if going on a spiritual retreat can be called a "crime") started to vomit all over the place — four grown boys projecting vomit at every point of the compass. They proceeded to vomit and dry-heave for the next several hours.

I had taken Castaneda's warnings to heart. I doubt if those boys ever read Carlos' second book, *A Separate Reality,* where all of this enlightenment occurred.

Russell and I decided to go walk about. Watching four men vomit was not what we had in mind as an enlightened event. So, we walked around The Hill. The scenery on The Hill in Boulder is fantastic. You have the big sky and The Flatirons. It was a great experience. As we walked down a street there, we heard this music playing behind a red-brick wall, so we both climbed the wall and dropped right into a party in progress.

Again, we were not eating or drinking anything.

We walked around this party and realized that everyone was speaking in a foreign language. We both thought that we had really stepped into another dimension of time and space. It was fascinating and disconcerting at the same time.

Finally, we found an exit and left the party.

The mystery was explained several days later, when we learned that we'd dropped into the foreign students' annual get-together.

After that event, we sort of split up, going our separate ways to talk to God.

I can assure you that, when you use peyote, you will most definitely talk to God. My only suggestion is to read Carlos Castaneda's books on the subject. Just because you own a few feathers doesn't mean that you can fly a plane.

Cheeseburger, Cheeseburger...

*U*pon my return from Australia in 1977, I moved back to Wilkes-Barre, Pennsylvania.

I needed a job. So, I went to the local job service, and they sent me to a detox center. It was called "Linc One" and consisted of a residential detox facility, for both men and women, with a program that lasted seven days. The center was manned 24/7, which meant that, every six weeks, there was a shift change. We worked 8 a.m. to 4:00 p.m., then 4:00 p.m. to midnight, and, finally, midnight to 8:00 p.m.

It sucked.

The day shift was the one most sought after, naturally, though the afternoon shift was still good enough for drinking. There wasn't enough time. Sure, the words "drinking" and "detox unit" should not appear in the same sentence, but, for me, at that time, it was of grave consideration.

One night, while working the midnight shift, I had a cocktail or two prior to showing up for work. My reasoning was simple: These people needed help, I knew how to drink, and, so, consequently, I was the man for the job.

At 3:00 a.m., we brought in a "client." We had a company car that we used for responding to bar owners' calls when they needed someone removed from their premises. Anyway, we brought in this guy, and he was perfectly smoked. While we were doing the Intake paperwork, the guy leaned across my desk and said, "If I didn't know better, I'd swear that you were half in the bag."

I leaned in close and responded, "That's why I'm on this side of the desk and you, my friend, are on that side."

In order to secure more funding from the state, I was asked to put together a slide presentation that could be used to sell our services to the moneychangers. With the help of Tommy Woods, a local radio personality who did voice-over, I went about the process of photographing and compiling a script that would extol the virtues of why this detox unit was necessary. We did just that, and it proved to be an outstanding piece of propaganda. The only problem was that the state claimed to be broke and didn't have any money for things like what we had to offer. I might add that, at that same time, Nancy Reagan was on television telling people to "Just Say 'No.'"

This was so typical: The government implements a program based around the concept of heroin addicts "just saying 'no'" to their addictions while they quietly remove all of the money to pay for the programs that may have made a difference. The Reagan years were notorious for doing that — denying funding for the same programs that they claimed publicly to be the answer to all of our problems.

But back to the story.

I saw the writing on the wall: This place was going under, and no amount of slide-show magic was going to re-inflate it. So, I showed up at the job center again.

This time, I scored.

The job consisted of working in a major state prison, running the "Arts & Crafts Shop," as it was called. It was a civil-service position, and my military record helped me to land the position. After signing a contract that basically gave them the right to allow me to be shot if I was unfortunate enough to be taken hostage, I was sent to a 10-week intensive training school and studied everything from Bomb Making 101 to Cell House Etiquette.

With that completed (I got a fancy diploma that hangs on my wall to this day), I was sent for by the big boss, the superintendent of the joint. It turned out that he wanted me to turn this shop into a money-making enterprise, producing woodwork, leather craft, and ceramic pieces that could be sold in the prison family rooms across the state.

I did just that.

There were a number of interesting stories that came from that position. Imagine going to work every day and passing through a number of giant gates, knowing that (a) the prison officials would not negotiate for your life and (b) you could be strip-searched at any time by the guards, looking for "contraband."

One day, I was at my desk in the shop, surrounded by 16 handpicked body-builders, who happened to be my employees. Three of them approached me with a request: Would I allow a person to come into the shop every week who could "service" these guys?

There was a men's room in my shop. Naturally, the door had been removed for security reasons. I said, "Yes," knowing that this was totally against the prison rules. But I didn't care. These guys worked for me, I was a civil servant, and the head of the security staff had once worked for my father.

The next week, "Cheeseburger" came into my shop, smiled at me, and proceeded to administer blowjobs to the 16 hardcore prisoners. I had them reposition my desk so that I could honestly claim not to have been a witness to these dastardly deeds.

One by one, my men would wander into the men's room and, minutes later, emerge smiling from ear to ear. Later on, it was explained to me that this was Cheeseburger's "job" in jail. He was paid a carton of cigarettes for each "service" he rendered, and he was just fine with the arrangement. In fact, Cheeseburger was fairly well off as far as inmates amassing wealth was concerned.

But, to this day, when someone asks me, "Would you like cheese on that burger?" I have to stop and think.

Note: Because I was a nice guy and all, one day, they approached me and said I could have Cheeseburger service me and that it would be their treat.

I politely declined.

Cheeseburger, Cheeseburger....

Death at the Drive-In Movie

*W*ay back when, we had souped-up cars. One thing about hot rods is the fact that the emergency brakes are never hooked up. Don't ask me why. That's just the way it was.

We had a couple of drive-in theatres. One was called "The Moonlite," but everyone knew it as "The Finger Bowl."

One particular night, I happened to be at "The West Side." This was the more respectable place, with better hot dogs and a more family-oriented atmosphere. Back then, all of the drive-ins had speakers on these metal posts that you placed in the back window of your rod. Nowadays — if you can even find a drive-in — they have "radio sound." So you just tune in their "station," and, Voila! Stereo sound.

I met this girl at the 15-cent hamburger joint, and we slowly got around to having a date — a night at the drive-in movie. I was prepared for any contingency, with my trusty "Prince" prophylactic slowly forming a bulging circle in my leather wallet.

Back then, a $5 bill went a long way. Gas was 19 cents a gallon, the drive-in was $1 a car load, hot dogs were 50 cents apiece, and beer, which came in quarts, cost 50 cents. You could get four gallons of gas, four quarts of beer, admission into the drive-in, and, while you were there, a couple of dogs "wit" or "witnot."

Anyway, I picked up my date, and we headed off to the drive-in. We actually watched the first movie and decided to do some "heavy petting" — as it was called — during the second. They always did that: showed the B-rated movie second because few patrons actually watched it.

My hot rod was a 1955 Ford Crown Victoria, which was a relatively rare car even back then. It was painted jet black and had a 312-cubic-inch "Police Interceptor" engine in it, with a big Holley carburetor. The gearshift was a three-speed Foxcraft shifter, and it was located on the floor, of course. No self-respecting greaser would have a gearshift on the column. Nor would they own a "slush box," as automatic transmissions were referred to.

So, we were making out hot and heavy, steaming up all the windows, and shaking the springs. I thought I was going to get a handful of titty and was in the process of undoing her bra clasp with one hand — an acquired art, I might add.

Not too many hot rods had bucket seats back then. Cars usually had a bench seat, but it was normally done up by an upholsterer. They were called "Tuck 'n' Rolls," the fancy bumps done in vinyl. Mine were done up in black and white, with some fancy stitch work in white thread.

Anyway, I was lying across the front seat with this sweet little thing beneath me on my fancy bench seat, when suddenly I felt this stabbing pain in my back. The girl had unscrewed my white Ivory shift knob and shoved me onto the metal rod sticking up out of the floor — hence the term "floor shift."

It was at this point that I glanced up and noticed that the stars were moving.

That meant my car was moving.

When my back had hit the shift lever, it knocked the car out of gear — the only thing that was keeping it on the side of the hill. The speaker wire grew taut and gave me just enough time to get up and step on the brakes.

Almost.

I was a little too late. The speaker ripped out my back window.

I carry that scar on my back to this day, a round

dent in my flesh.

Please understand: I was not a "crusher" type of guy. If a girl wanted to play around, I was game, but if she wanted me to refrain, I would oblige her — no problem. All she had to do was say something, like "Stop" — or even use the word "No." I would have understood.

The Great Outhouse Conflagration

*L*ike almost everyone I knew growing up, I had two grandmothers. Number one lived about a half mile from our house and was basically a real pain in the ass. The second one lived in New Jersey, which, back then, might as well have been the moon.

Once a year, my Jersey Grandmother, as she was called, would come to visit for a few days. I remember that she had natural red hair and the temperament to go with it. She also had a great laugh, but more importantly to the basis of this story was the fact that she and my dad hated each other. Jersey Grandma was a bit outspoken, and she didn't take kindly to some of my father's snide remarks.

Now, my father, also known as "The Big Duke" (a very apt nickname, I always thought), did not smoke. In fact, he hated cigarette smoke with a passion and would speak his mind on the subject whenever it came up. My Jersey Grandmother, on the other hand, was a smoker, and so the ground was laid for a Clash of the Titans every time she came to visit.

In order to keep the peace, I think my mother asked her to step out into the woods whenever she had a desire to light one up — at least until after dinner.

Back then, we were dirt poor. I addressed this subject at length in my first book, *a. Puzzled Existence.* Among other things that come with poverty is an outhouse, especially if you live on the side of a mountain, surrounded by trees. An outhouse can never be glamorous, although my mother did paper the wooden walls inside with a little rose-print wallpaper, and we kept the place tidy, with a broom in one corner and a bucket of sweet lime in the other to keep the bouquet at bay, you might say. I'm a poet and don't know it! (Actually I am a published poet. I published *NERVOUS READER,* 2013.)

Well, Northeast Pennsylvania is not known for its balmy weather. It is downright nasty at times. So my Jersey Grandmother did what any educated person would do under the circumstances — she went into the outhouse when she wanted to smoke a cigarette. That, in itself, would not have been a huge problem, even though The Duke would make a comment about how the outhouse would stink — an understatement, to say the least. But Jersey Grandmother took it one step further and dropped the still-lit cigarette butt down into the bowels of the outhouse (no pun intended).

Now back in those days, we couldn't afford toilet paper. That was a luxury when you have little to eat, so my mother would put her old Sears & Roebuck catalog in the outhouse, hanging on a stiff coat hanger. That meant that all of the paper — a fine pink tissue paper, I might add — was down there in the dark.

Well, the cigarette ignited the pile, and we had a meltdown — the outhouse caught on fire.

Using buckets of water from a rain barrel, The Duke managed to douse the flames, but he was fit to be tied. He ascertained exactly how the old outhouse came to be in this dangerous situation, and, when he confronted my Jersey Grandmother, she did what she always did when The Duke was a raving madman: She smiled.

To this day, we debate whether that was purely an accident or if it was meant to incite my father to the point of distraction. That answer, we will never know.

Steamboat Springs/July 21, 1975

I left Boulder, Colorado, on June 21, 1975 to drive to Logan, Utah, to visit "Doc" Murphy, who was studying at the University of Utah.

I was driving a 1964 MGB, with a little four-cylinder engine. I had the convertible top down, as it was beautiful weather — warm and sunny — as I drove up Clear Creek Canyon enroute to Utah.

The road started to climb in elevation. It turned cold and started to snow. With frozen fingers, I stopped to try to put up the top. It was extremely difficult, due to the fact that the ragtop had shrunk from being stored in the "boot," going unused for quite a while. My heater only kept the windshield from icing over. Other than that, there wasn't any heat in the car, so I wrapped myself up in an old Army blanket and pulled a watch cap down over my ears.

The steering wheel center had an emblem that popped off. Inside was a perfect storage area for about 25 joints. I pulled one out and fired it up.

The snow kept getting deeper. There were cars and semi-trucks stuck all over the road. I simply pulled it into second gear and kept the engine RPMs at a steady level, and drove on.

As I neared the top of the mountain, there was a sign that read "6 Miles to Summit." The snow, which had been building up under the car, ripped the exhaust pipe apart right under my feet. It made a horrendous noise, but my feet started to defrost.

I rumbled down the other side into Steamboat Springs, Colorado, and found a gas station that would allow me to use their lift. At first, they did not believe that I had crossed Berthoud pass, because, officially, it had been closed several hours earlier. They were still doubting me until they saw the snow packed under the car. They just stood there, shaking their heads.

I did this without any special tires or tire chains. Somehow, that little car just carried me over that pass without getting stuck. Naturally, once I started up that huge mountainside, I never slowed down — or even thought about stopping.

Near Death at Hoppy's Bar

*H*oppy had a bar in Courtdale, Pennsylvania. This place was a real dump, but it was popular with the shot-and-a-beer crowd. It was located in an old wooden house. The place was in really bad shape. In the men's room, you could see through the wooden floor down into the cellar, so drunken urine calls were treacherous, to say the least.

Well, Hoppy made enough money with his "skunky" beer and cheap liquor to buy a piece of land for a new bar location. The problem was that the land was embedded in the side of a mountain. But we at Goodman Excavators moved mountains, and that is exactly what we proceeded to do.

About four years later, Hoppy had his dream bar constructed, a cinderblock building with the most outrageous set of driveways any drinking bar — or "gin mill," as they were called — had ever seen in Courtdale.

The night of the grand opening, I was there with all of my brothers and probably the entire population of this little hamlet. We were in rare form, considering that all of the beer one could drink was on the house — something to wash down the *kielbasa* and *halushki*.

There was an older couple sitting at a small, two-top table near the bar. Suddenly, they began screaming, and we all turned in unison to see what the problem was. A huge wooden beam had dislodged itself from the ceiling and was in the process of falling onto both of them — a most alarming proposition, to say the least.

As it turned out, the "beam" was one of those styrofoam things that Hoppy had stuck onto the ceiling. His bar had that "exposed-wooden-beam" theme for all of the boozy hunters who hung out there. This thing just seemed to float down and just went "boink" on the old man's head. He was deeply embarrassed, but that didn't stop the place from exploding into raucous laughter.

If the beer hadn't been free, I'm sure they would have left Hoppy's in shame, but that didn't happen.

In Days of Old,
When Knights Were...

*O*ver to the South of our house on the mountain was an area known as "Greektown." This had nothing to do with Greeks. Actually, the real name of the town was originally "Gregtown," but I lived in an area where many things became misconstrued.

Greektown was made up of only a few extended families, and it had the reputation of fathers enjoying the wherewithal of their daughters from time to time. But, again, that was only the rumor on the street, and I can neither attest to it nor deny it. When you saw an old Buick filled with kids — well, let's just say it sort of lent credence to the story.

We would occasionally hire day labor from the pool of unemployed who lived in Greektown, and Ducky Shoemacher was one of these individuals. Don't ever tell him I called him "an individual," though — he will think it is an insult of some sort and come looking for me.

Needless to say, Ducky, like many of his fellow residents in Greektown, was not the sharpest pencil in the box. But he was a rather amiable type who was always smiling, and he did give a full day's work for his wage.

One afternoon, all of my brothers and I were standing in front of our garage, a rare occurrence on the best of days. We spied Ducky Shoemacher walking up the lot toward us. Sometimes, when the state inspection was due on their vehicles, people from Greektown would stop by and ask if they could "borrow" a muffler from one of our father's junker-car collections. They always promised to bring it back right after they got their sticker.

Naturally, that rarely happened.

So we thought that Ducky needed to "borrow" a used muffler or something along those lines.

He wasn't smiling when he walked up. My brother Bill asked him, "Hey, Ducky — what's wrong? You look down in the dumps."

As it turned out, Ducky had been out the night before with his girlfriend, and he related this story to us:

"I have been out all night. Spent most of it at the hospital, just waiting around for my girlfriend."

"Why was that, Ducky? Did you have a car accident or something?"

"Well, no. It's just that we were down on 'Baby Road' (this was one of the local love triangles where people went to make out), and I didn't have any rubbers, so I had to use a piece of plastic wrap, and it kinda got stuck in there."

We were half listening to this story when one of my other brothers said, "Wait a minute, Ducky. Are you telling me that you used a piece of Saran Wrap as a prophylactic?"

"I guess so, if they're the same things as rubbers."

At that point, all four of us were ready to start rolling on the ground in laughter when we realized collectively that old Ducky was truly upset about all of this. So we had to try to stifle our comedic outbursts and not hurt the poor man's feelings. As I mentioned, he was a good worker and didn't mind shoveling tons of dirt around for very little money.

But I guess we didn't pay him enough or provide healthcare — well, prenatal care, at least.

The thing that made this story so poignant for me is the fact that it occurred in the late 1960s.

Just think about that.

ZipLoc bags had not yet been invented, and Saran Wrap was relatively new. It was very expensive compared to waxed paper, which most sandwiches were wrapped in back then. I can just imagine what would have happened if Ducky had had access to a box of zipper-closure plastic sandwich bags. There probably would have been more little Duckies running around in Greektown.

Playboy Bunnies and Coalmen

*W*hen I was growing up, my dad was a coal miner. One day, he was buried in a cave-in and decided that enough was enough. He had been buried several times in the past, and my mother, now that she had four boys to care for, told him it was time to quit the mines.

First, he tried raising chickens. We had 300 of those bastards. Chickens are some of the dumbest animals I've ever had the dubious privilege of dealing with. They were dangerous, too. We had a bunch of egg-laying hens. When you have hens, you must have roosters to keep them happy, if you catch my drift. They had to have little, knowing chicken smiles when they came out from behind the coop with a rooster in tow.

When you went into the yard, these roosters would jump you because this was their turf, and they weren't going to share their hen booty with you or anyone else. They would jump up and claw at your face. Many a rooster mysteriously succumbed after scratching our faces. We told our dad that they committed suicide, and he, in turn, instructed our mother to make chicken for dinner.

Well, the chicken business didn't quite live up to expectations. So dad bought a coal truck, and we started to deliver coal. This wasn't your ordinary coal truck. It had a "high lift" body. The big box on the back would tilt and then go straight up into the air. Then, you used aluminum chutes to direct the coal into a customer's basement.

As my brothers turned sixteen, the legal driving age, the older one would drive, and the younger brother rode as helper. We were all two years apart in age — and that's how this worked. After a while, we had a thriving coal-delivery business, with more than 300 customers.

We hauled coal practically day and night. We even had special permission to leave school early every afternoon so that we could deliver coal. Our money was made per delivery — $1.50 for every ton we placed in someone's cellar. It was like piecework: The object was to deliver as many tons in a given period of time as possible.

My brother Mark and I were a team — we had it down to a science and really knew how to kick out the tonnage!

The only problem was our customers. We had to be polite to every one of them because there was a lot of competition in the coal-delivery business. We had this one customer named Mrs. Kenny, who owned a small neighborhood bar. As I mentioned in an earlier story, in our part of the country, neighborhood taverns were referred to as "Beer Gardens" or, simply, "Gin Mills." The problem with Mrs. Kenny was getting paid for the coal after we delivered it. Every time we went there, it turned into a tit-for-tat conversation between the two brothers.

"I went in the last time."

"No, I went in the last time — it's your turn."

"No, it's your turn."

Sort of like that.

When you went around to the back door to get paid, Mrs. Kenny would invite you in. She was always pleasant and would offer you a small shot of Mogen David wine in the Winter or a beer in the Summer.

Mrs. Kenny would make her way behind you and block the door. She would ask us about our mother and other brothers and ask again if you wanted a cup of coffee. You see, Mrs. Kenny wore a see-through negligee, and she was about 70 years old. She could probably tuck her breasts into her belt if she wanted to. That was why she never wanted you to just grab the money and run.

"It's your turn to go in there."

"No, it isn't. I did it last time."

Coffin Dodger

*W*hile growing up in Larksville, I had a set of grandparents who lived about a half-mile from our house. Their house was on a little street in among the dirt hills shoveled out by the coal company when they strip-mined the side of our mountain.

On Union Street, there were only three houses: One belonged to my grandparents, one to a family named Zuba, and the last house was owned by Coffin Dodger.

Nobody knew this guy's real name. He was a Russian immigrant who always wore bib overalls. Coffin Dodger had two sons, who were as weird as he was. They both dressed in shiny black suits with white shirts and black ties. These guys looked like funeral directors, even on a good day.

I used to get summoned by my Grandfather to do various chores around his house. Sometimes I had to crank the forge for his blacksmithing work. He made fireplace irons and stove pokers because everyone still burned coal in their kitchen stoves.

Sometimes, he would get a giant bag of coffee beans (my uncle Harry was the manager of a local A&P grocery store), and I would be told to go down there and grind them. I'd sit under the grape arbor behind the house with a huge glass jar, the bag of coffee beans, and one of those wooden grinders with the little drawer in the bottom. I'd fill the grinder on the top by sliding a little door open and then grind away. When it was finished, I emptied the drawer into the glass jug. This was how I acquired my lifelong addiction to coffee. While I sat there, grinding away for two to three hours, I chewed on coffee beans.

Coffin Dodger had a huge cherry tree in his front yard. This thing was massive. Every year when the cherries became ripe, we would look for excuses to go to Grandfather's house. The trick here was to sneak into Coffin Dodger's yard and climb up into the cherry tree without him seeing you, and that is what we would do. Once you were up in the tree, you could eat cherries until your tummy hurt. But, if he came out of the house, you were in trouble.

Now, Coffin Dodger would never look up into the tree as long as you were quiet and didn't bop him on the head with some cherries. He would stand in his yard shaking his fist and go on in Russian, *"Moc ya bac uoh babuska yost dah yon haloupkee, yesh ys spiff!"*

I never did find out what Coffin Dodger's real name was.

"You're Stupid — That's Why"

*M*y wife is from Pittston, a small city located midway between Wilkes-Barre and Scranton, Pennsylvania.

Now, the interesting thing about Pittston is that it's half Irish and half Italian. Mr. Buffalino used to live in Pittston along with a number of Gambino family members. I used to marvel at these guys. They'd be out there on weekends mowing their lawns in their baggy shorts and ginny t-shirts, mowing around those "Bathtub Madonnas." Are you familiar with those? It's simple: You take an old cast-iron bathtub and stand it up in the yard, pour cement into the bottom, and then put flagstone around it, being careful to follow the arch shape. After that is all finished, you buy one of those painted statues of the Blessed Virgin Mary and place it in there with a spotlight on it. That's a "Bathtub Madonna."

On the main street of Pittston is a real Italian butcher shop. I later found out that it was run by "Rocky" and his sons. I went in there one day to buy some meat. It was my first visit to this establishment. Rocky was behind the case waiting on me. I bought a couple of steaks and a few pork chops, and Rocky said to me, "Hey, would you like a nice pork roast? They're really fresh."

I replied, "Nah. Every time I do a pork roast, it comes out dry."

Rocky said, "Do you know why they come out dry? Because you're stupid — that's why."

I thought, *Whoa, there, buckaroo. Who the fuck are you calling "stupid"?*

Rocky walked around from behind the meat case and pulled something off of the rack. He handed it to me and said, "Here. This is what you need. Just cook it to 165, and it will come out perfect."

I still have that meat thermometer in my kitchen drawer.

The Disposable Lighter

*I*n 1968, I was halfway through an Associate's Degree in Advertising at a local community college. This college was brand new. It had been established in 1967 and located in downtown Wilkes-Barre. The powers that be had really deep pockets, so they could attract some of the best faculty that ever existed in our depressed area.

Two things happened that year: I enlisted in the United States Navy, and I bought a 1956 Thunderbird. This car was really special; it was a classic even at the time I purchased it. It had a factory gearshift on the floor. These were equally rare — a standard-shift 1956 T-Bird.

Naturally, I could not leave well enough alone, so I "souped up" the thing a little. It was given a new paint job — silver with a black landau roof. I put in a new engine, a 312-cubic-inch, big-block Ford, for which I had to borrow money from my mother — $500, which, in 1968, was a small fortune. I also installed two glass-pack mufflers and ran them through a set of resonators, which gave the car a really nice sound. There is nothing like the sound of a big Ford engine.

My friend Louie and I were business partners. We had a monopoly on the LSD trade in Wyoming Valley. He and I would rent cars and drive to either Boston or Hell's Kitchen in New York and buy a shoebox full of LSD. Orange Barrel, Purple Microdot, Sunshine, and, of course, the white, clinical variety. We made good money and kept everyone happy. Someday, I'll tell you about the night they screened The Beatles' *Yellow Submarine* movie in Wilkes-Barre, but not today.

Louie really liked hashish. He carried a ball of it as big as a golf ball with him at all times.

One of our stupid pleasures on Sundays was to drive out into the country and cruise up and down these small country roads in second gear. I would fly up one side of a hill and then roar down the other, just listening to those exhaust pipes growl. We did this for an hour or so because we did stupid things when we were smoking hashish. What can I say?

In 1968, a new French product came onto the market — disposable cigarette lighters. This was all the rage, and you had to comb the countryside to find someone who sold them.

After my experience in Iorio's Italian restaurant with the girl's hair, I wasn't going to take any chances.

This one was a beauty — red plastic — and it said "Made in France" on the bottom. Louie pulled out his hash pipe and dropped a boulder into it. Without looking at me, he said, "Hey, man — got a light?" I told him I did, and I added, "This is one of those new disposable lighters."

Louie huffed and puffed until he had the pipe stoking. There was a blue cloud around his head. Then he rolled down the window a notch and threw my disposable lighter into the woods.

I said, "Hey, Louie! What the hell did you do that for?"

Louie replied, "You said it was disposable, didn't you?"

I could not slight him on the logic in that statement, so we just kept roaring up and down the hills, listening to those exhaust notes.

You Going to Die, Kemo Sabe

*U*pwey, Australia, was a small town located in the Dandenong Mountains, about 18 klicks outside of the eastern suburbs of Melbourne. It was a popular mountain getaway back in the 1930s, a place where city dwellers went to escape the brutal Melbourne summer heat.

But when I lived there, it was more like an old whore with entirely too much makeup on. The place, though charming, was pretty beat. I rented a four-bedroom house there on a side street, near the polo grounds. Actually, they were the "Bowls," a grass-bowling sport popular there. The house was more than 200 years old and fairly well kept. It was on a side hill and had a beautiful windowed porch, which became one of my more successful art studios.

There were a few interesting stories associated with this house, one of which was the bona fide "cold spots" in one of the bedrooms and another dealing with the infamous "Huntsman Spider."

Today, however, I'll be sharing the story about the "Dunny House."

The house had a thoroughly modern kitchen and bathroom — very modern by Upwey standards, I'm sure. The bathroom had a nice sink and walk-in shower, but the toilet was located outside. It was called a "Dunny House." It consisted of a small building, complete with a door that had the proverbial crescent cut into it. Under the seat, there was a large, galvanized can with disinfectant in it. Once every week, at 5:00 a.m., the Dunnyman would come by in his big truck, empty the can, and place a fresh one under the seat through a small trapdoor located on the side. The reason for this was pollution. Obviously, the clay soil would not percolate a standard septic system, so this became their solution.

You must keep in mind that I grew up with an outdoor toilet for my first 13 years. (The complete story about that is in my book *a. Puzzled Existence*, published in 2010.) So, this arrangement did not bother me in the least. It really made sense when you think about it, considering the circumstances. But, my wife at the time — Wife #2 — was not impressed and reminded me how barbaric all of this was.

As was my routine, I would take a copy of

the *Melbourne Age* out there and sit, with the door open because there was a nice wooded valley to look at and no neighbors looking back. One day, I was sitting there reading the paper and ran across an article about the incidents of Brownback Spider bites being perpetrated on unsuspecting gentlemen sitting in their Dunny Houses.

The article went on to say how this species of venomous spider liked to live under the seats of Dunny Houses. And you must understand something: A bite from a Brownback Spider can kill you — it's like a snakebite. Your life might be spared if the poison could be sucked out in time. I can assure you, it would have been like a line from an old joke about Tonto and the Lone Ranger: *"You going to die, Kemo Sabe."*

My solution was to be found at the little hardware store in town. Four cans of Raid provided insurance against an early demise.

This Was Not a Triumph

*A*fter spending a few weeks in the Oakland Naval Hospital being treated for injuries sustained in Vietnam, I was discharged from the United States Navy at Treasure Island in San Francisco. The time was July 1970.

After a few more weeks in San Francisco, I made my way back to Wilkes-Barre and proceeded to settle in until my next plan was formulated. I'd served with guys from Australia on a few occasions in Vietnam, and they invited me to come down there and stay with them if I was so inclined. With nothing else on my busy schedule, I investigated and then booked passage on a tramp steamer to Melbourne a month later.

It was all set. I would travel to Australia and look up a few "mates" and settle down for a while. After Vietnam, I was ready to experience another country, and Australia was as good as any other.

What my plan did not entail was meeting a

woman.

One night, while I was drinking at a bar called "The Deep End" in Wilkes-Barre, I was introduced to a New York millionaire, and I decided to stick around in the States for a while longer.

Well, we moved in together, and all of my plans had to radically change. I sold my ticket on the banana boat and went out and bought a Triumph motorcycle. This thing was a beauty. It had less than 2000 miles on it, and it was just a sweet machine. The bike was a 500cc-high Piper with a single carb — just a nice, civil little bike that ran like a top.

I rode that machine through the Winter of that year, making runs out to Long Island, where my new squeeze was from — Stony Brook, to be exact. Naturally, I froze my ass off on some of those rides, but my bike never let me down.

The following year, at the beginning of Summer, I decided to sell my motorcycle and purchase a car. We'd been talking about moving to Florida, and it didn't seem feasible to ride a 500cc machine down to Boca Raton.

The bike was all steam-cleaned and polished. It sparkled outside of my studio that night. My friend Carl was coming up the following day to take the bike off my hands. I had the door open and would glance out every now and wonder if I were making a mistake.

A friend stopped by and asked if I would give him a ride over to Wilkes-Barre and drop him off at a popular late-night joint. So, I agreed — one last ride on my Chrome Buffalo before it was gone.

I dropped the guy at his destination and went around the Square in downtown Wilkes-Barre, got onto Market Street, and was accelerating through green lights to zip over the Market Street Bridge. There was one lone car on the bridge, waiting for a green arrow to make a left turn. All of my lights were green, but I used caution while kicking up through the gears. I finally decided that the coast was clear, and I twisted the accelerator to open the thing up. Suddenly, at the very last second, this kid, as I found out later, turned in front of me, saw my headlight, and stopped dead. His father's car was a huge Oldsmobile 88, which was as long as an aircraft carrier. I hit it dead center on the passenger side.

My bike crumpled, and I went flying over the car, landing on the Market Street Bridge, bouncing along on my helmet and knees. I came to rest and was lying there, looking up at the stars. There was blood running down my face, and I couldn't move.

A crowd of people gathered around. Where they'd all come from at 1:00 a.m. is one of those cruel mysteries, but there they were. I noticed that they were looking at me — but not at my face. I took note of this, but, under the circumstances, I didn't take it too seriously.

After some time, an off-duty nurse showed up and covered me with a blanket. The crowd dispersed, and an ambulance drove me to the hospital up the road. They spent a few hours picking asphalt out of my legs and patching me up until a doctor asked me if I could sit up.

With effort and some help, I sat up on the table to discover that my "Hip Hugger" jeans had split, and every seam in the crotch had gone in a different direction. I had been lying on the roadway with my crown jewels exposed for everyone to see.

As a protest of sorts and a way of putting to rest bad memories of standard-issue boxer shorts in the Navy, I'd gone without underwear until I had this accident.

You might say that this had been a lesson learned on the fly.

The Art of the Deal

*W*hen you grow up in the excavating business, you literally learn how to move mountains and fill in valleys. This is what we did for a living.

We would build lakes, sometimes roads through the woods, and, of course, we flattened mountains. When we did that sort of job, we would haul the dirt in trucks to a hole somewhere, and we'd fill in that hole. This was how you made money in excavating. Someone would pay to flatten a hill, and then someone would pay you to fill in their hole.

Once, we were involved in a job at a place called "Pringle Hill." We spent a week trucking dirt into a property and filled the entire front yard. Then, with one of our bulldozers, we graded the dirt so that the customer could plant a huge lawn, which they would have to mow for the rest of their lives.

On Saturday morning, I went down to the

shop, and my father was there. He told me to load up the l75C payloader and take it down to the job on Pringle Hill. A 175C loader is a huge machine. It loads a truck completely with just three big scoops. So, I didn't understand this order. We used this machine to dig out a lot of dirt.

So, I said to my dad, "Listen, I don't understand. We just spent the entire week hauling all of that material into that place, and now you want to start Monday morning and dig it all back out again?"

Patience was not one of my father's virtues. His impatience immediately shot into the red zone, and he said, "Don't you question me! Just load up the damn machine and take it down there! I pay you to work — not to run my business! Now get going!"

So, I loaded this giant machine onto a trailer and drove it down to the site. It was early — about 8:00 a.m., when I fired that thing up to back it off the trailer. Naturally, it woke everyone up, since most people slept in on Saturday morning. Suddenly the owner came running out of the house in his slippers and bathrobe. He ran up to me and asked me what in the hell I was doing.

So, I told him, "Look, pal. I don't get it, either. We just spent an entire week loading all of this dirt onto your property. Now, the old man tells me we are going to hog it all out, starting Monday morning. And I got my ass chewed when I asked about it. So, you talk to him. I'm just an operator."

As it turned out, the guy had threatened to stiff my old man out of a few thousand dollars. Later that morning, after he was properly dressed, he ran a check up to the garage. And later that day, I went down, loaded up that same machine, and brought it back.

Working on Cars

*D*uring the 1950s, Ford Motor Company introduced the Fairlane models of automobiles. They had a high-end version called the Victoria. It was a two-door coupe without a post. What that means is this: There isn't any metal between the front and back windows.

This looked really sharp. When the windows were down, it presented a nice, clean roofline. The car also had those little vent windows in both doors. You would open those, and they would direct an airflow over your person while you drove. This gave rise to the expression "2/40 air conditioner." This meant driving with two windows open at 40 miles per hour.

When I got the car, it had an automatic transmission. Though, today, I would not even think of having a stick shift, back then, a 16-year-old wouldn't be caught dead in a car with a "slush box," as an automatic was referred to then.

I decided to remove the automatic transmission

and install a stick shift on the floor, attached to a standard three-speed transmission. The only area I had to work in was a depression in the ground near a creek by our house. This proved to be a little difficult because creeks sometimes have water flowing through them — not the most comfortable position to be in when working on your back under a car.

What a nice-looking car! It was turquoise and white — a "two tone," as they called it —and it had a turquoise-and-white vinyl interior. It was very pleasing to the eye. But, more importantly, now it had a nice, shiny chrome gearshift on the floor with a white knob on it.

Really cool.

I would have attracted a lot of girls if it hadn't been for all the grease stuck under my fingernails. As soon as they saw that, I may as well have had a rhinoceros sitting on the floor — they still wouldn't go out with me.

The Conversation

In 1976, I was awarded a contract to write curriculum and teach in Melbourne, Australia. They flew me down there, and I stayed for a few years. My school was located on the outskirts of the city, and I had an opportunity to take a house in a small mountain town called Upwey.

At the school, I was told that I had to "do" at least one hour a week of physical education — in other words, watching a bunch of kids kicking a soccer ball around a wet field, while I stood there, freezing my butt off.

One day, while sniffing around my campus, I discovered a small, fully equipped weightlifting gym. It was dusty and dirty, and had not been used in years. I got permission and had my 15-year-old boys clean the place up. Then we were able to start a weightlifting program at the school. Since I'd been weightlifting personally for years, it was one of those win/win situations. It also qualified as my physical-education requirement.

Not far from my house in Upwey was a small commercial weight-training gym where I used to work out a few days a week. I have always used free weights to keep my weight in check, and this was the perfect place.

I arranged to have a bus provided by the Department of Education for the purpose of taking my class — or "form," as they were called down there — to this gym where I worked out. So we rode up there and did this. Then, we stopped at my house to have some "snags," which were Australian hot dogs, and beer at my place. These boys were blue-collar workers' kids, so they knew their way around a can of beer.

On the ride back to the school, I told a few off-color jokes. The weights, the beer, and the jokes were a form of male bonding. It helped give these kids, who'd come from hard families, something of a pleasant memory of their time in school.

One of my students was nicknamed "The Pommy." This was a mild insult because he was originally British, and "POM" stood for "Prisoner of Her Majesty." The acronym used to be emblazoned across the shirts of prisoners who were sent to "Botany Bay" as convicts way back when Australia was Britain's main penal colony.

Pommy said to me, "Sir, I have a little story for you. It's a conversation between The Big Toe and The Cock. One day, they were talking, and The Big Toe looked up and said, 'I live a dog's life. He gets me up in the morning, makes me stand in a puddle of water, and sticks me into the same old smelly shoe. Then, all day, he walks on me. When he gets me home at night, he shoves me into the same stinky slipper and puts me to bed, day in and day out.'

"The Cock looked down and said, 'You think you have it bad. He gets me up and slaps me around every morning. Then he puts me into those terrible jocks, and I go around all day rubbing my head raw. Then he gets me home, puts me in a wet suit, and makes me do pushups until I throw up.'"

Jesus Saves, and Peter Invests

*B*ack in the late '70s and early '80s, I used to drink a lot of liquor. In some circles, I was referred to as a "problem drinker." Well, I drank my second marriage away — though, at the time, I didn't think that it was any big loss. They told me that Vietnam had a considerable amount to do with it. Fighting in that war and surviving usually equated into a person with a drug or drinking problem.

Anyway, I was living in South Florida and operating a bulldozer for this company in Fort Lauderdale. One day, I met my new boss. The problem was that he wasn't new to me. I had worked under him at another firm, doing the same type of work — pushing dirt around.

At that other job, I'd saved his ass. You see, a good bulldozer man can make a boss look good or bad. A good operator can push dirt around fast and well, whereas some guys just work at a steady speed, which means time, and, in that business, time is definitely money.

So I saved him his job, and I guess he never forgot that little gesture. It turned out that this guy was now a born-again Christian, and he got it into his head that he was going to save me.

One morning I showed up on a job with two broken ribs. The night before, I'd gotten into a drunken brawl with a retired mob enforcer, and we'd beaten each other up over a woman — what else? My boss came to my job and had me sit in his car while he laid hands on me and spoke in tongues, asking the Lord to heal my ribs because he was behind on this job also and needed me to keep working.

It didn't work.

I could barely breathe, so I worked half a day and went home.

On another occasion, he invited me to a Christian Men's Breakfast. He used the logic that I would get a free meal out of the deal, so I went. After the breakfast, they laid hands on this guy and spoke in tongues for the purpose of selling one of his two condominiums. I got up and left. Naturally, he couldn't follow me out when he was in the middle of speaking in tongues and all.

The next day, he asked me why I'd left, so I told him that God had given us real estate agents for that purpose and that I thought it was a bit absurd to ask Him to sell a stupid condo.

He remained quiet for a while.

Then he asked me to go down to Miami to a ministry. The only reason I went was because this ministry had been started by an old Rock 'n' Roll singer named Wayne Cochran, known for his white pompadour and Miami ministry. And this intrigued me because I knew this guy's music — when he was a Rock 'n' Roller, of course.

So old Wayne preached fire and brimstone. Then he sang a few modified Rock songs that had "Jesus" in every line. I respectfully listened until he started pointing at me and screaming, *"You must be saved!"* He just kept pointing and shouting about my sinful ways and the demon liquor I was consuming.

So I got a little self-conscious and got up and left.

I stood out in the parking lot, smoking cigarettes and taking a sip or two of my half-pint, just waiting for the eight other born-again Christians to come out, all saved and full of joy.

Then, we all piled into this huge Chevy station wagon. It was one of those big nine-passenger vehicles that had the profile of a mastodon. Then we proceeded to drive up I-95 at a leisurely pace of 50 mph. As cars passed us doing 100 mph, they would all say stuff like "Hallelujah!" and

"Sweet Jesus Saves." The best one was, "Make Your Peace With The Lord Before You Die in a Car Crash!"

There was a lull in the advice to drivers, so I decided to tell them a story. It was the least I could do, seeing that I wasn't paying for fuel or anything like that. So, I told them this little story:

"One day, a guy died. He got into the elevator, and the operator looked at the paperwork and said, 'Buddy, you go up to heaven.' The guy told the man how he'd been good all of his life, how he'd gone faithfully to church, and how he'd never cheated on his wife. He'd basically warded off temptation at every turn, but he just wanted to see Hell. The guy in charge said, 'No, I can't take you there because I could lose my job. Your papers say, 'Heaven.'

"Finally, the man relented. He said, 'OK, I'll take you down there, but I'm only going to open the doors and let you peek. Then we are getting out of there.'

"The man said, 'Fine.'

"The operator took him down to Hell and opened the doors. A devil ran past, chasing a naked woman while they both laughed. There was a band playing dance music and a table piled high with all kinds of food.

"Finally, the operator said, 'That's enough. We have to get you up to heaven.'

"He went up there and opened the door. Over to the left were two people talking on a cloud. On the right was a woman playing a harp while floating by on another cloud.

"The lucky man said, 'Wait a minute! Where are the music and food? Why isn't there any dancing?'

"The elevator operator said, 'You don't think they're going to hire a band and a caterer for four people, do you?'"

Suddenly, there was total silence. You could have heard a pin drop in that Chevy station wagon.

Judging from the reaction of my fellow travelers, I could tell that I was never going to be saved — or make a living as a stand-up comedian at an evangelical church.

Kathy and the Cow

*S*oon after my second divorce, I met a girl named Kathy in Florida.

This girl was the real deal, a true South Florida chick. She had perfect white teeth and natural-blond hair, and she owned every form of marijuana and cocaine device that was ever made, meaning roach clips, one-hitters, and the like.

Kathy and I lived together for a while in a small neighborhood near Boynton Beach. This was relatively close to the ocean. We rented a set of rooms in a house that had been so eaten up by termites that they started to gobble up the cheap kitchen table and chairs I had moved into the place.

As time went on, I wore out my welcome in South Florida and decided to move back to my studio in Pennsylvania. Excessive alcohol abuse had a lot to do with that decision. Just my being involved with this girl was undoubtedly a product of my nefarious drinking habits.

After I'd settled in at my old studio, Kathy showed up one day in an old Chevy station wagon. It was a real clunker: The engine sputtered, the air conditioner didn't work, and the thing chirped a lot when you turned the steering wheel.

There we were, living in a one-and-a-half-room studio on State Street in Larksville, Pennsylvania. I slowly drank myself into the first of three psychiatric hospitals. They said I suffered from a disorder called PTSD, due to my combat experiences in Vietnam. While I spent forty-two days locked up in this hospital, Kathy used my studio and basically had sex with any guy who would come along.

She had this habit of starting an argument and then leaving for several days. I found out where she'd been gong later. But she'd always come back and give me a fungal infection. Now, she blamed that on the mountain creeks I used to use for my bathing needs. Of course, I never could quite accept that, but as long as my vodka supply held out, I really didn't much care.

After I was discharged from this hospital, my mind was clear, so I started to see things in a different light. Kathy's little escapades became rather boring, and I could see a change on the horizon.

One day, she received a handful of unemployment checks from the state of Florida. She had been waiting for these for several months. When they came, naturally, she had to return to Florida — alone. And she didn't see any reason to help with our living expenses over the past six months.

One night, we had the grandaddy of lovers' quarrels, and off she went into the night on one of her retreats.

At my father's house, she'd left a pile of stuff. By "stuff," I mean basically "junk" that she had acquired during her stay in Larksville. Some of this "stuff" was actually mine — things that she deemed payment for services rendered, like my Navy sewing kit and my Russian 35mm camera that I'd bought in Australia.

I wasn't drinking, but I still had some anger issues that would not be resolved until many years later. I sat in my studio, thinking about all of this, and I made a decision. I had to go see my farmer friend Bud.

I drove out to the farm with a couple of those white plastic drywall buckets you see strewn about construction sites and approached my friend Bud the farmer. I told him that I needed some really fresh cow manure. He took me into the barn and told me to shovel up a pile that was on the floor. But I said, "No — I need *really, really fresh stuff.*"

Bud said, "Oh, you mean the 'fresh-out-of-the-cow' material," and I concurred. He told me to hold a bucket under a particular cow's butt, and, sure enough, a stream of really fresh cow manure issued forth. I did this with a few other cows and thanked Bud the farmer.

I proceeded to my father's garage, where Kathy's stuff was stored under a blue tarp. Then I placed liberal amounts of this *really fresh* cow manure all over her stuff. I carefully replaced the blue tarp.

The next day, my dad heard someone cursing out in his garage and went there to investigate. Kathy was in the process of loading all of her stuff, which, of course, was scented with the smell of *really fresh* cow manure. Kathy appealed to my father, asking him why his son Jason would do something like this, and he responded by saying, "Well, you must have really pissed him off."

Then Kathy drove the 2200 miles down to Florida, alone, without the benefit of air conditioning, in her old Chevy station wagon, accompanied by the smell of a Pennsylvania dairy farm — a *really, really fresh* dairy farm.

A month later, I sent an FTD bouquet of flowers

with a card that read, "THIS RELATIONSHIP IS TERMINATED."

He Won't Be Home

There was a very popular bar in Boulder, Colorado, called "Potter's." It was right downtown across from the bank. Some afternoons, we would sit there drinking and watch the thermometer across the street, as the sun went down. The temperature would drop one degree per minute.

But that isn't what this story is about.

I was drinking at Potter's one night and met this attractive blonde. We made small talk, drank some liquor, and just basically spread a few thousand pheromones about the place until she invited me back to her place for the evening, and I, naturally, obliged.

Her apartment was on the second floor of a building, and, as I reached the top of the steps by her door, I noticed a pile of scuba-diving equipment in the corner. So, I asked her, "Are you a scuba diver?" She said no, that her husband was a commercial diver on the oil rigs. The equipment was his extra stuff. But, she added,

"He won't be home."

I was still a little skeptical because I didn't like dating married women — for this very reason.

We went in, and one thing led to another, and we ended up naked on the bed. My doubts had diminished with the sexual bliss — until, that is, I heard the front door open.

She jumped out of bed, threw open the window, and told me to jump out. I went over and looked. I realized that we were on the second floor, but at that moment, this huge man walked through the door holding a Hawaiian Sling.

I don't know if you are familiar with this piece of underwater equipment. It is a spear gun that uses big rubber bands to shoot a very lethal spear. Divers use them for spear fishing and shark protection.

As I flew out of this window, I heard the *Thunk!* of the spear impale itself in the windowsill just under where my scrotum had been a few seconds earlier.

Fortunately, I landed in a tree, which broke my fall but rendered me a bleeding mess on numerous areas of my body. Soon thereafter, a few articles of clothing and a shoe sailed from the window before the shouting started. I covered my manhood as best I could and made my way to the car to make an expeditious getaway.

Afterward, the thought did occur to me that, in the police blotter, it would have read: NUDE MAN SHOT WITH SPEAR GUN WHILE TRYING TO ESCAPE LOCAL APARTMENT BREAK-IN.

When you stop to consider that the nearest ocean to Boulder is about 1000 miles away, the irony washes over you like a wave.

Naked Aggression

I was at my studio one hot summer night. Outside, my trusty little British sports car sat waiting. It was a 1964 MGB that I had completely rebuilt in anticipation of a trip out to the West and maybe on to California.

Barbara was a woman who used to stop by the studio. She'd married a son of wealth from an old Pittsburgh family. I normally did not like messing around with married women, but not because of some high-handed moral conviction. It was more like personal survival. But she assured me it was alright because of the loose relationship that they maintained — one of those New Age-type marriages.

It was hot, even at midnight, and, not long after came the knock on my door. Barbara was out, and she wanted to play. I obliged her with the suggestion of a ride in the country in my sports car, with the top down and a half-gallon of fairly decent wine I had stowed in my back room. With all of that in mind, we set off into the night.

Not many people realize how hot those old MGBs used to get. The exhaust pipe, fresh from the engine, ran under my right foot, just below the accelerator. On my trip to Utah in this thing, my shoe was melting and stuck to the floor. That's how hot the floor used to get. This, in turn, warmed up the rest of the interior below the waist and made riding somewhat uncomfortable.

For this reason, I suggested that we start removing our clothing, and that is what we did.

Piece by piece, our clothes left our bodies until we were both sitting there in my blue-leather bucket seats as naked as the day we were born.

This seemed to solve the problem of the hot interior, and we drove on, enjoying the country roads about three in the morning. Barbara sat there with the half-gallon jug of wine between her legs. She said that it helped cool down an otherwise heated portion of her anatomy, and I had no reason to doubt this logic. It also made it very convenient for taking occasional pulls on our jug of wine.

We were driving through a little town called Orange, Pennsylvania, when it happened: A police car started to follow us and, sure enough, as soon as I got to the outskirts of town, he gave me the blue lights. But, if my memory serves me correctly, I think they were red back then. At any rate, I pulled over.

Slowly, this officer walked up to the car. In Orange — a town of about 46 people — there wasn't a lot of high-profile crime to solve on a daily basis. So, he could afford to take his time getting to the car. I remember that he was carrying one of those huge flashlights that double as a club when necessary. And it had this long, red-plastic lens sort of thing on it. Let's just say that it glowed red for some reason. I remember from my Navy days that, when we were at sea, we had to wear red goggles before we went up on deck, in order to acquire night vision. This could explain the color and length of the officer's flashlight.

My date thought that this was just about the funniest thing since The Three Stooges. She was sitting there naked as a jaybird (whatever that expression means), roaring with laughter, and a half-gallon jug of wine between her legs.

Meanwhile, ol' Fearless Fosdick came up to the car and made a rather lengthy and thorough investigation of our joint nudity. Then he sputtered, "What the hell do you think you're doing?"

So, I explained our dilemma and the engineering of a 1964 MGB automobile and how my exhaust-system configuration added to the already-oppressive heat situation in my car, which, in turn, had precipitated the removal of all of our attire.

He interrupted my explanation by saying, "You can't drive through my town in that shameful state."

Barbara countered with, "Why not? We aren't doing anyone any harm. Plus, if you check your watch, you may notice that it's almost 4:00 a.m."

I cringed at her outburst, certain we would be spending a night in their local lockup. But her legal expertise seemed to confound this officer, because his face turned the same color as his big, long flashlight, and he just stood there, shaking. Finally, he spun on his heel and stormed back to his police car.

The only thing that bothered me was the fact that he spun out and kicked gravel all over the bonnet of my automobile.

Death by Traffic Signal

*L*iving in Boulder, Colorado, was one of the best experiences that I have ever had.

I ended up there after a trip to Logan, Utah, to visit a friend of mine who was studying at the University there. (See the story in this book called "Steamboat Springs/July 21, 1975.")

In Boulder, I rented a nice bachelor pad on The Hill, drove an MGB sports car, and landed a job operating heavy equipment with a small company called Boulder Excavators. Usually, I operated backhoes and bulldozers, but, on occasion, they would send me out as a truck driver. The boss once said, "Look at it this way: You are the highest-paid truck driver in Colorado right now."

Boulder was where I became a union operator. I was forced to join the AFL-CIO as an Operating Engineer, one of the highest-paying union jobs in the entire country.

Boulder Excavators had two mobile cranes.

These are the giant things with a whole bunch of tires going down the side and a big metal box-like structure sticking out from the front. You could drive them to a job, though it was preferable for them to be stationary, set up on blocks, with their crane sticking up into the air.

I was not a crane operator, but they did press me into service occasionally as an "oiler." The oiler's job is to drive the crane to the job site and sit around all day watching stuff being lifted up to the top of a building under construction. Years ago, an "oiler" did just that — oiled the crane from time to time. But modern cranes don't require oiling, so I pretty much just sat around.

Every large crane comes with a separate small truck called the Jibe Truck. Their function is to carry the extra crane segments, including the jibe, a small piece of crane that goes on the very top. We had to do this because all of the crane parts could fit on the mobile unit except the one that stuck out about 25 feet.

We were in the downtown area, right next to the courthouse. It was a four-way-stop intersection, with red lights on every corner. In Boulder at that time, they mounted the traffic signals on separate poles sticking up from the sidewalk. They weren't overhead, like they are now.

The light turned green, and I was about to make

this very long swing with the crane when the Jibe Truck driver called me on the two-way radio. He said, "Quick — look over at 3:00 o'clock. Check it out." So I looked over my right shoulder. A young girl was walking down the steps, and the wind blew her dress up over her head, providing us with a view of some of the nicest-looking legs any construction worker would ever want to lay eyes on.

At that moment, I was making my swing and not really paying any attention when I felt this series of bumps. When I turned around, there was the crane, knocking off the last of four traffic signals. Three were already hanging upside-down by their wires, and the fourth, to my horror, just fell on the ground.

Jibe Truck told me to keep on going and that they would stop to settle the problems with the police. So I just continued on to Denver and parked the crane at the job site for the next day.

When I got back to the yard, I was told that the boss wanted to see me — naturally, I assumed that he would give me my walking papers. I entered his office; he was sitting there behind the desk, all serious and basically pissed off. He asked, "Was she that good looking?"

I replied, "Yes, she was."

Then, to my relief, he told me that that's what

insurance was for.

Speed Kills

*O*n one of our early trips to Europe, my wife and I were traveling around using Eurorail passes. We were allowed unlimited train travel in the first-class cabins anywhere the rail system went.

We pulled into Koblenz, Germany, late in the evening. It was one of our longer days of travel, and we were both pretty tired. At the Information kiosk, they directed us to a taxi and gave the driver instructions on where to take us. After a short journey, the taxi pulled up to a rather drab-looking building, and we stood there just looking at it — another one of those clean-but-boring places to stay.

So, I paid the driver, and we lugged our suitcases into the building. When the door opened, it turned out that we were on the Esplanade, and across the Rhine River stood the famous Stolzenfels Castle. It was breathtaking. The place was all illuminated from below, and the river water just shimmered with light. Below us were the grassy areas and walkways that held small cafes where we'd be having breakfast in the morning.

One morning, I walked alone up the river for a while and ran across the boat docks. As it turned out, there were two ways of traveling up the Rhine and into Nuremberg. One was the slow boat, which would take close to four hours. The other was a Russian-built hydrofoil, which made the trip in 45 minutes. I inquired and learned that, because we had first-class Eurorail passes, we could take the Hydrofoil for only an additional $25.00.

My mind was made up. I booked passage for the next day.

As a surprise, I told Teresa that I had booked us passage on the river to Nuremberg —but I didn't tell her exactly how we would be doing it.

The next morning, we boarded the craft, and it wasn't until they left the dock that it became apparent that this thing could really haul ass! We roared up the Rhine River.

My wife had every intention of photographing the many castles along the way, but she soon realized that that would be impossible because we were going too fast, and she didn't have any high-speed film — *really high-speed film.*

Louie's Missing Hash

*I*n the late '50s and on into the early '70s, both Ford and Chevy marketed a car which was half sedan and half pickup truck. Ford called theirs the Ranchero, and Chevy named their version the El Camino.

Now, even though I am a staunch Ford man, the El Camino was the better design. My oldest brother just happened to own a 1964 Chevy El Camino.

In the mid-'70s, I was planning on returning to South Florida to continue my education. It was Summer, and I didn't start school until the Fall. I needed an automobile but didn't want to buy a car just then. But, suddenly, my brother agreed to rent me his El Camino. He claimed that he really didn't need it because he had another car and a Ford pickup truck. I accepted his offer and became the lessee of a nice El Camino.

It was a sweet ride. It had a bench seat, and the back was open, like a truck, but it retained all of the attributes of a nice car. It was a real pleasure to drive, with a small V8 engine and automatic transmission. This little machine was just right.

Louie and I had been friends for many years by then. We'd met in college. He went to Wilkes University, and I attended Luzerne County Community College, but I used to hang out at Wilkes, and that's where we spent our time.

Louie liked marijuana — he smoked the stuff all the time. In fact, later on in his career, he was diagnosed as the first person to be clearly addicted to the stuff, although that subject is off message for now.

Louie and I would hang out, and I was the one with the ride. We would take my rented El Camino and go driving around out in the country, smoking hash and just looking for adventure. Personally, I never much cared for pot. I preferred hashish, and Louie would oblige me on occasion with some nice black hashish, or opiated hash, which was even more of a treat.

One night, we were out patrolling the country lanes in the El Camino, and Louie pulled out this giant ball of hashish. This hunk was bigger than a golf ball. It was really nice stuff, too. So, we drove around getting stoned. I don't think that bong went out once during the course of the entire evening.

Coming up on midnight, I saw Louie looking around the car. He started searching the entire cabin until I asked what the problem was. He told me that he'd lost his ball of hashish. I stopped, and we both looked around inside the car, to no avail. So I suggested that we stop at my family's garage in town and do a thorough search.

At the garage, I got out the drop-cord light and started looking under the seat, but it was difficult because of the shape of the cabin on the El Camino. Louie suggested that we remove the seat.

I went in and brought out the air gun and sockets, and then we added the creeper into the mix. A creeper is a low chunk of wood with little wheels on it. You use it to lie on while you scoot yourself under the car. I had to go under the car in order to get at the bolts that held the seat in. Naturally, that required the use of a floor jack to lift the car high enough to squeeze under it. Finally, after a bit of a struggle, we removed the entire front bench seat.

There wasn't any hashish to be found.

I asked Louie if he might have dropped it somewhere else, and he assured me that he had not.

Meanwhile, the local police stopped by, wanting to know what was going on. It was well after midnight, and you'd have thought that we were removing the engine, judging by the amount of equipment lying around. I assured them that everything was under control, and they went away satisfied.

I couldn't very well have told them that we had misplaced our giant ball of black hashish. That would have strained our relationship dramatically.

Finally, I told Louie that it wasn't there — that hash was not in this automobile. He started rummaging around in his pockets — and produced the same ball of hashish.

The moral of this story is to strip-search your friend when he tells you that he's lost his ball of hashish.

Better yet, don't even go out with friends that own a huge ball of hashish.

Nudity vs. Romance

*D*esperation led me to do desperate things in South Florida.

I was a student at Florida Atlantic University and paying all of the bills myself. Times were tough. I found myself eating baby food.

Allow me to explain that. Baby food came in sealed little jars. You needed only a teaspoon to eat them with, and, at that time, they were 10 for $10. No heat, no refrigeration — just protein and a little something to keep my stomach from growling.

I found myself doing anything for money. I started writing articles for the campus newspaper, which paid $30 apiece. I became a Residential Assistant; that paid $60 a month and came with a private room near the rear exit and a private telephone. And I worked part time on campus with the various maintenance departments for $4.50 per hour. Then came a glorious opportunity: The Art Department was looking for people who would model nude for their life-drawing classes. My rationale for taking that job was the fact that I was a student of art and one day would be teaching life drawing, Plus, it paid $10 per hour. In 1975, $10 an hour was really big money.

For this position, I was on call, which wasn't a problem because I had a telephone, compliments of the university. So, when I got the call, I went to work. They had me doing some rather dubious things. I remember modeling for the Photography Department, and this one woman had me hanging out of trees, among other things. I finally realized that she was taking pornographic-like pictures of yours truly, so I had to walk off that particular job.

One day they called me for the life-drawing class. In the center of the room, they had an elevated platform. On top of it was a cube made out of strips of wood. My job was to lie inside this cube and change positions every few minutes when the instructor said, "Time."

I was in the process of taking 18 credits per quarter, working toward a degree in Art Education. In my travels around campus, I would see this one particular girl. For some reason, I found myself attracted this person, so I tried to be where she might show up — at the library, in the cafeteria — anywhere on campus where this person might hang out. You could say that I was working on brand recognition, if I may borrow an expression from my commercial-art training.

It seemed to be working until one particular day. As I rolled around inside this wooden cube, it became apparent that the huge air-conditioning duct was right above me, blowing chilled air down into my immediate area. The instructor called, "Time," and I rolled onto my right side.

There, sitting about 10 feet away was the girl of my dreams. It was at that same time that I realized, after catching a quick glimpse, that my penis was all shriveled up. It was like a tiny little fireman with his little red cap on, just peeking out from his little forest of hair. You could say that I was mortified, but, being the consummate professional — a somewhat embarrassed consummate professional, I might add — I forged on through the hour-long session, tiny little penis and all.

I had to soothe my aching ego with the thought that I was now $10 richer, though not a dime would be spent on a date with that particular girl.

Doc Murphy's Skull

*W*e had contracts with several cemeteries around the West side of Kingston, Pennsylvania.

They would call, and I or one of my brothers would run down with one of our backhoes and dig a grave for them. Most cemeteries have charts that tell you exactly where the graves are. This comes in handy when you are digging between two vaults in a family plot. Also, somewhere along the line, the state had mandated the use of concrete vaults. Every casket had to be placed inside one of these long, narrow concrete boxes. I can tell you this: Every vault that I had reason to tamper with was full of water, usually foul-smelling stuff that would pour out if you accidentally bopped the thing with the bucket and it cracked. But, that isn't necessarily the gist of this tale.

The Shawnee Cemetery was non-denominational. It was run by the town and not affiliated with any church or for-profit burial company. For that reason, there weren't any charts in this place.

When we dug a grave there, anything could happen, usually in the form of strange things appearing on the growing pile of dirt.

The caretaker at the Shawnee Cemetery was this old, grizzled guy. He wore bib overalls and leaned on a shovel while standing next to my machine. I can't recall him ever using his shovel, but, then again, it made a good leaning post. On one occasion while I was digging, when I dumped the dirt onto the pile, a rib cage rolled down the bank and came to rest practically at his feet. He used his shovel to toss the thing back onto the pile. I idled the machine and asked what we should do about this. He casually told me to bury it in the dirt so no one would see it, which is what I did.

During this time, I was studying art at a local community college and had a friend named Doc Murphy. When I related the story of the errant rib cage, Doc asked me to keep an eye out for a skull. He was a little weird and wanted a skull for his studio. Doc used to paint while listening to Wagner operas. He worked in oils and did really strange, Dali-esque scenes, muscled figures flying around in the background. So, with that in mind, I didn't even think twice about his request for a skull.

Sure enough, a few weeks later, Shawnee Cemetery called and needed a grave dug pronto. I jumped on the machine and drove down there to perform this service. While I was digging, I threw a few bones onto the dirt pile and thought about Doc's request for a skull. So I started digging a lot more gently, hoping to pull a nice skull out of the ground.

After a few minutes of digging, I decided to stop and take a break. Naturally, the old caretaker was standing there, leaning on his shovel. We started talking about things until I brought up the issue of the bones that kept popping up. He stood there, hiked up his overalls, spit out some tobacco juice, and said, "You see, young fella, the problem with these bones here is that most of these people died from the plague. Yep, back in nineteen hundred and eighteen, a whole bunch of people were buried here."

As soon as I heard the word "plague," I decided that old Doc would have to order a skull from some place in China, because I wasn't even going to get down from my machine, let alone start digging around with my hands.

Then the old-timer continued, "I often think about this when I'm digging here. Some of those plague bugs can lie dormant in the bones for

100 years or more."

Well, that did it.

I wasn't going to set foot in this cemetery ever again, and Doc Murphy would have to live without his skull.

Something Foul at the Tree Line

*B*oulder, Colorado, was one of the best places I ever lived in.

I may have mentioned this before: I owned a nice English sports car, had a neat bachelor pad on "The Hill," and worked as a union operating engineer, which equated to big bucks in the mid-1970s.

One of the nice things about Boulder was the active lifestyle. It was just a pleasure to live there, and that made it very easy to do all kinds of things outdoors.

My friend Russell was the younger brother of my first wife. He was a student at The University of Colorado in Boulder and lived above me in this big old house on The Hill. Russell was an active kind of guy, so it didn't surprise me when he asked me if I would be interested in a hike up to the tree line — a hike to a magical lake where we would spend the night and return the next day.

Well, that day came, and we drove to our jumping-off point somewhere in the Rocky Mountains outside of Boulder. It was a typical Boulder kind of day — just beautiful. We hiked all day, crossing streams by using fallen trees as a bridge, and stomping across snow packs, dressed in cut-off shorts — just all-around great hiking. I was in charge of accommodations, and Russell was in charge of our provisions.

We trekked close to 12 hours to reach Reindeer Lake, a wonderful setting up past the tree line. We were surrounded by vistas of the great Rocky Mountains. We pitched camp, gathered firewood, and settled in before it grew too dark.

On my trip out West in my MGB, I had borrowed my brother Mark's two "Mummy Bags."

These were government-issue sleeping bags that were rated at 20 degrees below zero. They sort of came to a point at the foot end, hence the name "Mummy Bag."

Russell brought out our provisions — an aluminum pot and a big, industrial-size can of refried beans, the type that institutions buy for famished orphans. I asked Russell if that was all of the food, and he said no, the spices were in the bottom of his knapsack because the plastic sandwich bag had broken. So, there he was, heating up this mass of mud and spicing it by dumping his entire knapsack into the pot.

I went over and noticed that there were huge trout swimming around our big rock that jutted out into the lake. And I was determined to snag one for my dinner.

It was to no avail. I tried everything. I unraveled string from one of the Mummy Bags and my knapsack. Then I found one small safety pin in the bottom of my other bag. Then I went about the task of finding a piece of suitable bait by overturning rocks and tearing a few stumps apart. Nothing worked. I dangled that hook in front of the trout's nose, but he wasn't in the least interested.

So, there we sat, packing away one spoonful after another of this spiced mud. I could see the trout swimming around from my dining vantage point, and it did nothing but fill me with a gnawing desire, left unfulfilled.

After dinner, Russell started talking about the grizzly bears that roamed these tree-line environs, and I assured him that, after getting into those Mummy Bags with what we'd dined on, no self-respecting grizzly bear would get within 100 yards of our little outpost.

Winter Burn

*W*ith the onslaught of Winter in Boulder, I signed up with a gym called "Harvey's Fitness Center," a small, segregated place for men and women. Harvey had a real nice, tight weightlifting gym, with a nice sauna and some tanning booths. Two were tanning beds, and the other was a stand-up thing you stepped into and closed the half-circle door of tanning lights behind you. The machines took quarters. I think you got seven and a half minutes for 25 cents.

After a good workout on the weights and a refreshing 180-degree sauna, in the dead of Winter, Harvey would shovel all of the snow into a big pile in the back yard. You would run out of the sauna bare-naked and dive head-first into the snow bank. He had a little sign that warned of heart-attack potential.

Well, I did all of that — sauna, snow bank — and then I went back and decided to work on my tan. Back in those days, I sported a really nice tan all year round. I could tan so well, people thought that I was a minority after a while.

There wasn't anyone in the place, so I decided to tan in the nude. I wanted that "uninterrupted" look — no lines of any sort. I popped a few quarters into the stand-up machine, walked in, and closed the door. Now, I did have the presence of mind to wear eye protection — those little white goggles with the circular dark lenses in both eyes, but the thought never occurred to me to provide protection for that area down there — you know, my manhood address.

Oblivious to all else, I tanned away, standing there, just thinking about Potter's nightclub and the girls I would meet that evening.

Unbeknown to me, my Johnson was being par-broiled, and he made his distress known to me later that evening. My poor little penis went through the entire process. It got beet red, then blistered, and after a while, it peeled like crazy. During this entire time, the thing hurt like hell. What a stupid thing to do to my dick!

If I'm not mistaken, an entire month transpired before my pecker was returned to service. I thought I was going to have to sign up for workmen's compensation. Can you imagine the conversation — trying to explain the nature of your injury to some bespectacled state bureaucrat?

"What is the nature of your complaint?"

"Well, my cock is all burnt and sort of shriveled up. This prevents me from doing much of anything, your honor."

The one good thing that came out of all this was the answer to a mystery that had plagued me for years.

Do you remember the situation in Shakespeare's play *The Merchant of Venice*, when Antonio was to pay back "…a pound of flesh…"? For years, I labored over that dilemma. How do you get a pound of flesh without drawing a drop of blood? This was the answer:

You sunburn the hapless Johnson until it peels. Then you harvest that bit of flesh. Repeat over and over again until you have an entire pound. There's your answer. An upright tanning booth and no thought for the consequences.

Shylock should take note of this epiphany.

Howard Harvey and Jesus

*A*t that same gym in Boulder where I used to lift weights and suntan naked, the monthly plan came with a perk: For $30 a month, I'd get unlimited use of the weight gym, the sauna, and, of course, the tanning booths that took quarters. The Overall George Hamilton look was extra.

What was included in that $30 a month was a complete body rubdown. Howard was a Seventh-Day Adventist. He was also a health nut who didn't eat meat and went up into the mountains to pick the herbs he used in his infused-oil formula — the oil that he would rub all over my body during my weekly rubdown.

I had set Wednesday as my night for a rubdown. I would go and work out with the weights for an hour or so, take a 45-minute sauna, and then have Howard give me a body rub. It was more like a massage than anything else.

Howard would start on my neck and head. He would do my vertebrae, crack my neck, and then work over my shoulders and the backs of my legs. He was somewhat rough in technique, but I liked that sort of massage — one that had some real zip to it.

Then Howard would have me turn over. He would reposition my towel and start on my arms. He'd work his way down to my lower legs. Here is where the problems would come into focus.

A Seventh-Day Adventist is supposed to preach the word to someone every single day. It's in their contract. Now, I didn't mind Howard preaching Bible verses to me at all. What I did object to was the timing of his repertoire.

You see, Howard would work himself into a born-again frenzy, and just when he reached my toes, he was in full swing, talking about Jesus. He would yank on my toe and scream out, "Jesus!" Who was born in Bethlehem? Jesus! Who died on the cross for our sins? Jesus!"

Just as he got to that word, he would pull my toes.

"Jesus! Wow! That hurt, Howard!"

One day, while Howard was massaging and preaching, I stopped him just when he got to my feet. I said, "Listen, Howard. I don't mind you preaching to me, but could you keep Jesus out of my toes for a change?"

The Chinook Tragedy

*L*eonard used to be a downhill racer of promise. He was training for the Olympic Games when tragedy struck. One day, during a high-speed descent on the slopes, he fell and broke his back in several places. When they moved him in his full-body cast, it bent; his back healed with a curve in it. The doctors — the same ones who had caused this problem — told him that he would never walk again.

When I met Leonard, he was riding a 10-speed bicycle and walked bent to one side. He told me that he would one day ski again, and I believed him.

Leonard didn't make too many friends in Boulder, where everyone was quite beautiful. Most people there would not be caught dead hanging around with a crippled guy like Leonard. When you think about it, we are all disabled in some way or another. So I befriended Leonard. I used to take him up the mountain to Nederland to go drinking beer and then drive back at breakneck speed, wheeling around corners with the tires screaming. Leonard loved every minute of it. Leonard liked speed.

One day, we went out to the reservoir with Leonard's Sunfish sailboat. He was going to teach me how to sail. A Sunfish is a small fiberglass boat with a relatively large sail. They were fast in the water. We were out there for a few hours while Leonard demonstrated different techniques for tacking and, basically, the operation of any standard sailing vessel.

I was at the helm, just putzing along, when I noticed Leonard tense up. He was looking in the direction of the Rockies, which were right behind me in the distance, all snow-capped varieties of them. He pointed and yelled out, "Chinook — it's a damned Chinook!" Of course, I had no idea what he was talking about until I turned around and saw the entire mountain range covered in snow and dust. A very big wind was coming down over the mountains.

For some reason, the Rocky Mountains channel wind all the way from around Seattle. It flows through the mountains and ends up over Boulder and Denver as a really strong current of air. Sometimes it will reach speeds of more than 100 mph and will tear up anything in its path that isn't nailed down. The Indians called it a *Chinook*, which translates as "a big wind," or "Brother Wind With the Big Lungs." (I just made that up, but you can Google it and find out, although you undoubtedly get the picture.)

We were out in the middle of this huge reservoir, with nothing but flat water between us and the leading edge of this killer wind. In other words, we were in deep trouble.

"Larry" told me to switch seats with him.

In an emergency, Leonard would just become "Larry" instead of "Leonard." It was easier to say and type. Larry just didn't feel that I'd had enough hours at the helm to handle this kind of high-speed sailing, and I concurred.

Let me tell you: When that wind hit us, we took off like a rocket. Leonard and I were literally racing across the water. I could swear we were doing 60 mph within seconds.

Leonard was in his element. He had this huge smile on his face, coupled with a look of dire concern. We were in trouble, and both of us knew it. If we were to flip that boat over, there was no telling what may have occurred. But he was competent and sailed that thing for all it was worth.

We were pointed right at the parking area and concession stand and traveling very fast. "Larry" shouted to me, "When I tell you, pull that center board up as quick as possible." The center board is the keel of a sailboat. It sticks down into the water about four feet. It is the thing that keeps you from flipping the craft over when you make a sharp turn. Ocean-going sailboats have a keel that is packed with lead to keep the craft upright during a gale.

And a gale it was. That boat seemed like it wasn't even touching the water — we were skimming along on top of it. As we approached the shallow water, "Larry" yelled out to pull the center board, and I yanked this board straight up. At that moment, we went right up the "beach" and across the gravel, carving a path through the stone. The only thing that stopped us was a green Volvo. Our boat crashed right into it, leaving a substantial dent in the rear door.

Leonard and I had survived, although the Volvo owner didn't seem too impressed. I told him to have the dent fixed and to send me a bill.

Hole in One

*D*allas Penitentiary, also known as the State Correctional Institution at Dallas (S.C.I.D.), is part of the Pennsylvania prison system. Dallas is located about 18 miles South by Southwest of Wilkes-Barre, Pennsylvania, in the rolling hills between mountains belonging to the Appalachian range on the East Coast.

In 1978, I was working as a Drug and Alcohol Counselor at a residential detox unit in Wilkes-Barre when the call came. The employment office contacted me and asked if I was interested in a teaching job at S. C. I. D., and I said, "Yes."

I went through the hiring process right up to an offer that I accepted, but, before they would allow me to sign the contract, I had to meet with a tribunal of officers from that prison. They asked me the same question three times: How did I feel about the fact that they would not negotiate for my life under any circumstances?

After this grueling session, I signed the papers,

and everyone shook my hand.

As it turned out, I wasn't going to be teaching anything. The superintendent wanted me to open a money-making arts-and-crafts shop in the education building inside the compound. I was to hire up to 16 inmates, establish a working production shop, and produce goods for the inmates' relief fund. Or should I say, the sale from which would benefit that fund. It was the high road toward some prison reform, though I didn't really care. The job was a civil-service position and paid handsomely, not to mention the slew of State benefits. So I agreed to the task presented to me and operated this area successfully for more than a year.

My meals were provided by the state. We ate the same food that the inmates did, only we had our own dining room. This meant that, if there was a rumor that someone had pissed in the food, we were ordered to eat it anyway. The biggest spark that could set off a riot in prison concerned the food that was served.

I was connected to the Education Department. This meant that I wore regular street clothes. The security people, turnkeys, and screws wore blue uniforms, and the maintenance people wore khaki uniforms.

The Security Department was run like a military operation. There was a Captain of the Guard, Lieutenants, Sergeants, and so on — a rank and file based on any typical military branch of service.

Here, I had an in. The Supreme Commander of the Guard used to work for our family business. Although everyone thought I had used the "Bubba" system to land this job, the truth was that my educational qualifications and the fact that I had veterans' preference actually made the difference.

The first six months were pretty intense. I had to restructure the existing arts-and-crafts area, add materials, and hire a workforce. My highest-paid man earned 16 cents per hour, which as far as prison was concerned, proved to be really big money.

My employees and I turned out a number of products, from leather wallets and purses, to nice, inlaid wooden cutting boards, to cheesy ceramic Christmas trees with little colored lights glued onto them, but they all did the job. We kicked out the stuff, and they sold it at the visiting center. We did so well that we actually exported handmade goods to other prisons to be sold in their visiting centers.

Things were on an even keel.

I worked a strange week. My days off were Sunday and Monday. I ran the regular shop from 8:00 a.m. to 4:30 p.m. every weekday, Tuesday to Friday. But, on Saturday, I had to open the shop to anyone who wanted to work on an arts-and-crafts project of their own. This was due to a successful inmate lawsuit that had been brought against the prison, preventing the institution from barring the population from utilizing this area on Saturday.

The problem for me was the fact that the shop had to be open from 12 noon until 8:00 p.m. on Saturday, and this made for an uncomfortable work week for me, because working in a major prison and drinking liquor were quite synonymous.

One evening I went to the officers' dining room for dinner. I used to check the menu and then decide if I wanted to have dinner at work. Most of the food was all carbs — thick sauces made from flour and a lot of potatoes. But, again, due to a lawsuit, they had to serve pork chops and cube steak a certain number of nights per week, and these were the meals that I would take advantage of.

I was sitting at a table eating alone, when an old Sergeant asked if he could sit with me. This guy had worked with my old man in the coal mines and had nothing but good things to say about him. I was Billy Goodman's son, and that was good enough for him.

After he sat down, he said, "Goodman, I've been here more than 25 years."

I told him that I knew that and asked him what the trouble was.

He went on to say, "I thought that I'd seen everything in this hellhole, but last night just took the cake."

"All right, Sarge. Tell me what happened."

He went on to tell me how they had to do a cell check late at night. When they checked a certain cell, an inmate was missing. Not an uncommon occurrence. So he proceeded to say, "Damn it, Goodman, we went down the tier, and, sure enough, there was our man lying on top of this guy in the rack. So I told him to get up — that he had to go back to his cell. When he got up, we saw that he had a centerfold from a *Playboy* Magazine draped across the other guy's ass, and, damn it to hell, Goodman, he had cut a hole in it…."

A perfectly good piece of slightly chewed fried pork chop went flying across the dining room floor.

300-Foot Rope, 20-Foot Fence

*T*he State Correctional Institution at Dallas was surrounded by two 20-foot fences. In the history of the place, there had been only two known successful escapes, both of which ended in the arrest and re-incarceration of those involved. Now, this prison houses more than 1000 inmates. When I worked there, they kept the racial balance of the inmate population even, at 50% White and 50% Black detainees. Up until that time, there had never been any attempt by Black inmates to escape.

One of the main reasons for this was the perpetuation of a myth by the Security Department concerning the disposition of the deer population in the forest surrounding the prison. The guards, or "Screws," as they were called, told them that these deer were carnivorous and that anyone caught out there in the woods would be ripped apart and devoured by these hideous beasts. Because many of these inmates were from the larger cities around Pennsylvania, this story went unchallenged for many years.

One escape that I was told about involved an old man. The Captain of the Guard — who had worked for my father years earlier — related the story to me.

This old man ran the perimeter of "The Yard" for more than three years, and no one paid any attention to him. One day, he went about his business of jogging around The Yard, and, in one quick moment, he ran right up and over the two fences and scurried into the woods. They eventually caught him, a few hours later, but the prison's policy regarding the perimeter fences changed after that.

Back in the late '70s, the concept of macramé was a big fad. Artisans would weave rope, usually hemp, into three-tiered hangings that incorporated round glass pieces woven into the design. These were then suspended from the ceiling, and plants or various objects were placed on the "shelves" as a decor item. This technique and viability was not lost on the inmates or on the prison guards.

Actually, the prison guards really would take some liberties with security. I had guys bring me wooden replicas of their favorite pistols so that the leather-makers could fashion holsters for them. At first, I was shocked until I checked with Control and found out that they were aware of this. Naturally, I wasn't comfortable. It is said that John Dillinger escaped from a prison using a "gun" fabricated from a bar of soap. Here, I had several wooden guns floating around my shop.

One day, an order came into my shop, and in it were two coils of hemp rope. This stuff was about a half-inch thick, and there was 300 feet of it. Naturally, I displayed an appropriate level of alarm. What the hell was 300 feet of rope doing in a prison with 20-foot-high fences?

The guards from C Block assured me that everything was just hunky-dory, so I allowed this huge Black inmate to carry it over to his cellblock.

Well, about a week later, the Captain of the Guard was showing off his prison to some dignitaries from the state capital when they happened upon the recreation room of Cell Block C. There, in a corner, was the same huge black man, standing with 300 feet of macrame rope at his feet, quietly weaving knots into a hanging piece.

After they had taken me off of the rack, I was suspended by my thumbs for a few days.

Several days passed before I could convince my operatives of my innocence. Finally, they allowed me to leave the dungeon and return to population.

Shooting Waters

If you want to hide from the FBI or even the KGB, join the carnival.

I'm serious. Just get a ride down to Sarasota, Florida, and find one that is hiring.

Carnivals and carnival people are the modern gypsies of the United States and probably every other country that they operate in. Once you become part of their "family," no one will ever find you, because they will not turn you in. The Feds could show videos of you walking out of a Wal-Mart loaded down with hot goods, and they would not recognize you. That was my experience.

I finished a Bachelor's Degree at Florida Atlantic University and returned to Pennsylvania. I had promised my girlfriend at the time that I would buy a sports car and take her to California.

While hanging around Larksville trying to figure out where all this dough was going to come from, I ran into an old friend. Greg had just bought a carnival game. It was called "Shooting Waters" and consisted of a small house trailer-type of thing on wheels, with 14 high-powered squirt guns mounted on a countertop.

The idea was to travel around the circuit of Pennsylvania and upstate New York with this game and make a ton of money — something of which I was in short supply at the time.

My position was general helper and barker on the game. Greg paid me a daily wage, plus all of my expenses while on the road. We traveled throughout the state, playing all of the Grange fairs and various bazaars — anywhere we could part someone from their hard-earned quarters.

The object of the game was to fill a clear plastic tube with water and try to get a ping-pong ball into a little red basket that was attached to the back of the tube. Whoever got their ball out first was the winner and got a "Rat." If that person was lucky enough to get their ball into that basket, they were awarded a large "Plush." The only thing that distinguished a "Rat" from a "Plush" was the size.

We didn't give too many of those away. The basket was just a tad larger than the ball. Getting the ball into the basket was sheer luck. I know, because I tried many times.

We would often live behind the midway

for three to five days — however long the fair lasted. Sometimes our neighbor, who had the .22-caliber rifles with the bent barrels, would often ask me to "rube" for him. I would go up and shoot a bunch of bullets, and he would announce me a "winner." Then he'd hand me a big ghetto blaster. I would turn it on and walk away, usually around back, where his wife was waiting. This was simply to entice the crowd into spending money on a rigged game.

When it was time to work, we called it "Going On," as if we were performers, which, when you think of it, we were. I would make references to Watergate and offer up the "inside tip" that this wasn't a game of chance — it was a game of skill. This would bring them in.

Inside the game, we had about four feet of space. Both of us used those canvas carpenter belts to collect the money and make change. In both corners, we had two low wooden stools where we would sit while the game was in progress. Under the counter were the controls for the squirt guns. These were plastic replicas of the famous .45-caliber Colt 1918 pistols. There were pressure fittings under there that controlled the pressure of the guns. We had to make sure that no single gun had more pressure than the others, or the game would not be equal — and people noticed things like that.

One night, these punk kids decided they were going to mess with us. Unbeknown to us, they stood at both ends, and, when we weren't looking, poured Coca Cola onto our stools, so that, when we sat down, our asses got soaked. And this is exactly what happened.

The next day, we were working on the game, cleaning things and just checking everything for the evening performance when we spotted the same kids. We quietly turned up our two guns each to maximum pressure and lured the boys into our "killing zone." When they got within our range, we opened up with a gun in each hand — two high-powered water pistols that could shoot more than 75 yards. We tracked these guys as they tried to escape and soaked them from head to toe.

It was a case of sweet revenge for a night of working with a wet ass.

At the Laundromat

*W*e lived in Charleston, South Carolina, for about six years.

Our place was an old wooden beach house on Folly Island. We occupied the entire top floor, with a deck and a front room that was surrounded by windows. It was there that I set up my studio.

Directly across the street was a vacant lot. The old-timers told me that a small amusement park used to sit there but that it had been taken out by a hurricane many years ago. Just beyond that was the Atlantic Ocean. It was a beautiful location.

Fortunately, we moved on before the developers came in. They built an apartment building across the small street, completely blocking the view of the ocean from the house. We drove down the street many years later, and our house looked like an old whore without any makeup on and wearing a see-through negligee.

But, while we were there, it was idyllic and a great place to do artwork. The only drawback to the place was the noticeable absence of a washer and dryer. For that, we had to drive up James Island to a small strip mall to do our clothes. The gym I used to lift weights at was not far from this location, and so, the task of laundry usually fell on my shoulders.

Most days, I didn't have any problems at the laundromat. I went in, loaded up a few washers, and sat back, reading the paper until it was time for the dryer. But some days, it became a difficult situation. I don't want this to sound like prejudice, but my problems began when this hoard of Black women would converge on the place. They would park right in front of the place in the handicap spaces and unload a ton of dirty clothes. Then, they'd use at least 10 washing machines apiece.

Normally, I could deal with this. It was the drying cycle that became a problem. These women would take up every folding table in the place. This would not have been bad if they had just folded their clothes and moved on — no, that would have been too easy. They would fuss around and talk up a storm, stopping the folding process every minute to tell a bigger story than their counterparts.

It would drive me crazy. I had to stand in the back, trying to fold clothes while standing up, until, one day, I got an idea.

People generally would agree that my wife is well-endowed in the chest region — not that I go around trying on her underwear. Let's just say I know this from experience. So consequently, her bras are on the expansive side, and some of them do not have rounded cups. You could almost say that they come to a point. But, in my limited folding space, they were getting in the way of folding the pillowcases.

I placed one of her bras on my head — one of the pointed varieties — and the cups stuck out like a Viking helmet. I even tied the straps under my chin for effect.

These women underwent a physical change. First of all, the talking ceased. When I glanced over, they were all standing there staring at me.

Then, the miracle happened.

They started moving their clothes from the tables closest to me, and quickly folded away until they were all out of the door.

Anytime I went to that particular laundromat, I used to place a bra on my head at the very start. That way, no one bothered me, and I could have any machine in the place without even asking for it.

Those Damned Hippies

I spent a summer working as a barker in the carnival. Most of the time, I was away on the road. We toured all of Pennsylvania and most of upstate New York, playing the county-fair circuit — and, I might say, we made a lot of money.

On my days off, I rebuilt an old MGB. It was a 1964 model, a very rugged and dependable little English sports car. When it was completed, I intended to drive across the country, mainly to explore US Highway 1, in the coastal regions of California.

The carnival season ended, and I put the finishing touches on my car. It was all loaded up. I had two US Army-issue sleeping bags, a case of Rolling Rock Beer for my friend Doc Murphy in Utah, a set of blank 8-Track tapes, and my round, deerskin duffle bag.

I recorded eight 90-minute tapes with all different kinds of music on them and painted them black. There were no distinguishing characteristics on them at all. The reasoning behind this was twofold: The cabin of a 1964 MGB is quite small, and, while you are traveling, especially alone, you couldn't go searching through a box of tapes looking for something specific to listen to. This system took all of the guesswork out of it.

Another modification was a custom steering wheel. It had a better grip surface than the original, and the center emblem popped out. Under that emblem was a space that would hold about 25 rolled joints. It was a perfect hiding place that no one would think to search.

With everything in place, I decided to set off and drove West. After a few miles, I decided to stop in to see some friends of mine who lived out in the country. It turned into my big send-off. We actually ended up having an impromptu, extemporaneous party, with plenty of pot and Boone's Farm Apple Wine being passed around. If you decide to drive across the country, don't leave on a weekend, and do not stop at your hippie-dippie friends' house, either.

Early the next, morning, I was on my way, but right before I backed out of their drive, Elaine came running out with a small box that contained freshly baked brownies in case I got hungry on the road.

Things went fairly well. It was a beautiful day, and my little car was running like a top. So, I just drove West, traversing Pennsylvania, and then onto Ohio. It was when I was just about 50 miles out from the Indiana border that I remembered the box of brownies. So I pulled them out and started to munch away. At first, they tasted a bit strange. It seemed like they had some sort of heavy fiber in them, but they tasted decent, and I was pretty hungry.

While I was driving along in Indiana, I noticed that things were starting to strike me as being really funny. A big bug hit my windshield, and I burst out laughing. Plus, I just felt really good. So, I decided to eat another brownie. This one tasted even better.

As I was chomping away on this thing and staring straight ahead at the road, I got that feeling that someone was watching me, and, sure enough, when I turned my head, there was an Indiana State Trooper, driving alongside me in the passing lane, at the same speed that I was doing. It dawned on me that I must have had this most-ridiculous grin on my face from all of the laughing.

I didn't know what to do, so I just kept on eating my brownie and driving. I knew that he knew there was something amiss in this little sports car, but he just couldn't put his finger on it. This lawman drove alongside me for what seemed to be a dozen miles, and then he just sped up and left me in the dust.

Yep — you guessed it: You can't trust those damned hippies — and don't drink or eat anything they give you.

Night at the Carnival

A typical day working at the carnival went like this:

Greg and 1 would wake up around 9:00 or 10:00 a.m. We would make some breakfast on our little camp stove and then go and check the game. As I mentioned before, the game was called "Shooting Waters," and it consisted of a small house-trailer-like thing with 14 high-powered squirt guns mounted on a counter. We would clean the game, fill the water tanks, and just do basic maintenance.

After that, we were free for a few hours. Usually, we had to go and find someplace where we could take a shower. That became a very creative endeavor in itself on most days. We didn't "Go On" until around 5:00 p.m. By that time, there were people roaming around the midway, and we would gather up a few dollars on the early crowd. The place didn't start really hopping until after it got dark. Then things really picked up, because this game was a game of skill. It attracted a lot of people.

The only thing rigged were the baskets that the ball had to go into in order for the customer to be awarded a really big "Rat." That was what we called the stuffed animals — Rats. They came in two sizes — big and really small. These things were cheap pieces of crap, but what would you expect for a 25-cent investment?

The crowd would generally thin out around 10:30 or 11:00 p.m. We would sit on the bunk beds, counting and bagging quarters. Sometimes we would bag up to $1800 for one night's take. Like I said, we made a lot of money, and it was all cash. After the loot was counted and put away, we sat out back in our folding deck chairs, drinking beer and shots of gin. Don't ask.

Greg liked gin, and because everything was included in my tenure, I wasn't going to argue or buy my own liquor.

One night while we were sitting out, one couple next door were having one of their regular arguments. This couple was something else. He was skinny as a rail, and she was quite big. But the main thing about this girl was that she wore T-shirts without any bra. Her shirts all had something silk-screened on them, little sayings like, "Candy is dandy, but sex won't rot your teeth" — little pearls of wisdom like that.

So, they were arguing about the draft. They slept in a car, an old 4-door Chevy. The rear door was all stove in. This allowed cold air to seep into their boudoir, and she wasn't going to stand for it any longer. So, the next day, they went to a local junkyard and bought another door.

That night, Greg and I were in our chairs, getting hammered on beer with gin chasers, and we were observing the activity next door. The boyfriend was out there, trying to bolt this junkyard door onto his Chevy. The problem was that the door was for a Buick. The sheet metal was completely different. We tried to explain this to the poor guy, but he kept insisting that they said it was the correct door.

Somehow, he got the thing to stay on, but it was absurd. The door was a completely different shape.

There must be a moral to this story somewhere, but I cannot, for the life of me, think of what it could be.

I just hope that this couple refrain from having too many offspring.

The Big Deceased

*N*eville and I were dispatched to a church in North Melbourne. We were told to take the hearse and show up there at a certain time for what was supposed to be a two-man carry. One of the services that Tobin Brothers provided, in keeping with funeral directors the world over, I suppose, was providing pallbearers if the family did not have anyone specified.

We drove up to the church and smoked our usual two cigarettes before going inside. We quietly entered the church, and I heard Neville let out a sigh. I asked him what was wrong, and he pointed to the coffin and said, "Look at that — it's an oversize coffin." Naturally, being new to the death business, this fact didn't immediately mean anything to me.

There are little tricks — some would say techniques — to being a professional pallbearer. One of them was the signaling method. The leader, or person in the front, would tap the bottom of the casket with his fingernail, in a sequence of taps, determined in advance, that would indicate when to lift the casket from the trolley it rolled on. Then, another tap or two would indicate when to begin walking.

It worked fairly well. You would be surprised how well those taps would carry through the material of the casket. When you went to lift, you placed your hand flat on the bottom of the coffin. Then, with a loud tap, you would both lift at the same time so that the coffin was raised up evenly and not lopsided. That would have been in bad taste and considered embarrassing to the owners of the company. They did run a very respectful and tight business. At every location, they would place these automatic shoe-shine machines at every door. We were required to shine our shoes (black only — there isn't any brown in the funeral business) every time we left a facility.

They had assured us that this job was a two-man carry. On the way to the church, Neville made a few comments about them saying that and then, sometimes, finding out otherwise. No matter what, we had to carry that coffin out of the church. It was going to happen.

When Neville gave me the signal, we both lifted — and nothing happened. The poor deceased woman inside was extremely overweight, and, between her and the coffin, this package must have weighed in excess of 400 pounds. Yet Neville and I were assigned the task of getting it out of the church by ourselves.

After a few attempts, we got the casket up on our shoulders. Normally, we would support it with just our hands and use our shoulders as a backup. But this time, we had to rest the thing on our shoulders.

We struggled down the steps and barely got it into the hearse, almost dropping it as we lowered it down.

Neville and I were a mess. Our backs hurt, our shoulders had permanent dents in them from the coffin profile, and we were just exhausted. It was a long walk from the foyer of the church, out the door, and down a flight of steps to our vehicle. As I drove, Neville checked the clipboard to see if it was a dirt burial or a cremation. If it was a cremation, it would have been slightly easier on us because the distance would have been shorter.

In Australia, we did anywhere from four to five funerals a day. We worked our asses off, usually 12 hours a day. Out of five funerals, three of them were usually cremations. Based on my experience, I quickly learned that Australians preferred cremation to dirt burial. I don't know why, but that was the consensus.

Neville started muttering under his breath, and I asked what the problem was. He said that this was going to be a dirt burial. He went on to say that it was going to be our bad luck that the grave would be located a half-mile from the road.

Well, guess what? As I drove into the cemetery and we checked aisle and row signs, we located the grave. Off in the distance, almost 100 yards away, was the tent and an open grave. We were in big trouble.

During the Australian summer, the ground is dry as a bone — no pun intended — in a cemetery. It just never rains — that all happens in the winter. Plus, the sun beats down all day. Usually, the ground is like concrete. As we walked — or, should I say, stumbled — my heels were leaving imprints in the dirt and what was supposed to be grass. I am talking about real holes in the ground — that's how heavy this coffin was. I don't know how we did it.

What I do know is this: When we got back to our branch office and checked the records, we discovered that the woman weighed 438 pounds.

Mistaken Identity

The police in Melbourne, Australia, never stop a hearse — this is a fact.

For ten weeks, I worked in the funeral business and drove the hearse on most assignments. Tobin Brothers used big V8 Chevy vehicles for good reason: Speed.

Melbourne is absolutely huge. The city is crisscrossed with major four-lane roads, and it can take more than four hours to drive across the entire city. All of the cities in Australia are like that — BIG!

Another thing about Australia are the drivers. They are perfectly insane. I had colleagues tell me that they were nice, reasonable people until they got behind the wheel of their automobile. For some reason, the road turned them into maniacs.

Most of the crashes that I ever saw in Melbourne were spectacular — cars lying in bits about the roadway and always an ambulance carting away the occupants.

Neville and l were just finishing up a long day. It was approaching four o'clock, and we had started at seven that morning. When I signed on with this company as a "casual laborer," I was told that the job would be part time. Well, if my paychecks were any indication, I worked a minimum of 12 hours a day, six days a week.

It was brutal. We worked in the Australian summer heat, wearing grey suits with powder-blue shirts and burgundy ties. Every part of my shirt was soaking wet except the triangle where my tie was located. The other thing that was really hard to take was the smell of flowers. They piled all of the flowers into the hearse on both sides of the coffin. These would be transported to the cemetery to be placed on top of the grave.

Neville and I crawled into our branch office after this hellacious day to be told that we had to deliver two caskets for morning church services. This was a bit of bad timing. We had dates that evening and were supposed to meet these girls at 8:00 p.m.

We got into the hearse, and Neville checked the clipboard. He started cursing like a sailor until I stopped him and said, "Tell me where we're going first." He held up the paperwork and said, "Jason, these churches are on opposite sides of the city. It will take hours to make these two deliveries."

With the two caskets on board, we set out. I was driving at a steady 100 mph, laying on the horn for people in the fast lane. We raced to the first church and prepared the client. This, in itself, was no easy task. We had to get out a trolley and wipe it all down — the chrome had to glisten. Then we had to load the casket onto it and roll it into the church. Once we set it up in front of the altar, we had to wipe the entire casket down, using a wood polish. There couldn't be one fingerprint on the casket, or there would be hell to pay.

After the first stop, I roared back onto the freeway and sped toward our next objective, a church on the other side of the city. The same process was repeated: Wipe down the trolley, roll the casket in, and polish it with wood cleaner.

After that delivery, we high-tailed it back to our branch. There wasn't any time to change. We had to show up dressed in our matching grey suits.

Great, we thought, *new dates going out with two uniformed undertakers — Neville and Jason, just your two friendly ghouls.*

The next morning, I walked into our office, and I could hear the shouting. I asked Ian, a fellow undertaker, what was going on, and he told me that Neville had been called onto the carpet. It had something to do with the previous night's delivery. I waited until he came out. He told me to step outside while we had a smoke and could get away from prying eyes and ears.

What had happened was this: We, apparently, had placed the Catholic in the Protestant church and the Protestant in the Catholic church. No one realized what had happened until they were well into the praying over these dearly departed individuals — and then all hell broke loose.

If you are familiar with "The Troubles" in Ireland, you will know the type of animosity that exists between Catholics and Protestants. Hell, it carries all the way to Australia. The country was founded by convicted prisoners deported by the British Crown, mostly from Ireland.

I wonder what position God had taken during all of that praying?

Sex to Die For

necrophilia (nek-ro-**fee**-lee-ah) n., an erotic attraction to corpses.

*W*e had special vans for doing hospital pickups. They were Ford vehicles referred to as "panel vans." There were two seats up front with a partition and a closed rear cabin.

Neville and I came in one evening from doing funerals. We parked the hearse and went in to punch our time cards when the boss spotted us. He said, "Not so fast, mates. I have another little job for you two. I want you to take a panel wagon, go down to Royal Melbourne hospital, pick up a client (that was a nice way of saying "body"), and deliver it to the Dandelong branch."

Naturally, we both started to use some very unsociable words to describe our feelings, but, deep inside, we both knew we needed the extra money because our new girlfriends were proving to be expensive nuts to crack. So, we headed out into the darkening night, driving to a hospital to pick up a dead person.

When we got there, an orderly showed us down to the morgue area and pointed to a couple of gurneys with white sheets on them. He said that the one over there was our charge, the one by the wall. "You can open those doors and back your vehicle in for the loading. I have to leave, and I will let you two have at it."

With that, he turned on his heel and left.

Neville walked over and pulled at the sheet. It slid off in one fluid motion to expose a beautiful woman. This girl was beyond a "10" — she was not only pretty, but she also had a body most women would have, well, died for.

Neville and I stood there motionless; we were stunned. This poor girl was just absolutely gorgeous. After what seemed to be an eternity, Neville pointed to the hose on the wall and said, "Jason — that one is hot water." Again, we just stood there and stared at this young woman lying on a stainless-steel table.

Very abruptly, we came out of our little trance. We both started to act like buffoons, jabbering away, making no sense whatsoever:

Well, we better get the van, and blah, blah, blah.

As it turned out, she was 23 years old and had died of an overdose. What a waste of a life —

not to mention the complete package that came with it.

Whenever I think of that incident, I thank whatever powers-that-be that I did not go through with anything inappropriate. I know, beyond a shadow of a doubt, that I would have lived with that bad decision until my own grave called.

What would you have done?

Feedin' and Washin' Up

The funeral director ran the entire funeral in the field. He was basically our boss. He would ride to the church with the family in the mourning coach and stay with that family until the entire funeral was over.

Usually, the director, dressed in tophat and tails, would be at the church before we showed up. Our schedule was so crazy that we would be finishing one funeral and on our way to another one in progress. They had the timing down to a science. I don't remember ever being late for the next funeral.

I usually drove the hearse. At first, I thought it was the better job, but, after days of sitting in there with all of those flowers, I would become a little green around the gills, as they say. To this day, I cannot stand to be around a bunch of funeral flowers, although, today, most people don't use that many flowers — and this suits me just fine.

Neville and I showed up in the hearse and backed it up to the church door. We got out, and there was the director with one other guy. This was going to be a "three-man carry," as they call it in the trade — three pallbearers instead of four. Of course, on that one job (see the story "The Big Deceased," elsewhere in this book), it was just Neville and I with a very large woman.

We all stood out in front of the church, smoking cigarettes, and the funeral director was by the door. Ian or Neville would ask him what was going on inside. The funeral director opened the door a crack and peeked in. He said, "He's feedin' 'em." This meant that the priest was giving holy communion. After a while, he would peek in again and say, "He's washin' up." This, of course, would mean that the priest was going through the ritual of cleaning the chalice and replacing it back into the tabernacle. Finally, the director would look again and tell us, "They're payin' the tab (collection basket going around) and gettin' ready to thank the cook…." This would mean that we would have to straighten our ties and button our jackets because, very soon, we would solemnly walk down the aisle single file and prepare to lift the coffin onto our shoulders and carry it out to the hearse.

Barefoot in the Park

*A*s mentioned in one of my other stories, most Australians preferred cremation to dirt burial. At least that was what I observed years ago while working in the funeral industry in Melbourne.

The crematory was something else completely. We would back up to an overhead door. There was a slot in it that would open, and in went the coffin. It rolled on a series of small rollers, the type of which were used in the bottling industry. One person could move a heavy casket with ease.

The casket would be rolled onto a platform that was controlled from a central location. The operator could dial in what religion was needed, and the altars would spin around to the correct one. This was accompanied also by the correct music for that particular faith. The coffin was placed on a platform that used hydraulic cylinders that would lift it up into place, while the music played. Of course, then, after the brief ceremony, it would lower again, very slowly, for effect.

Once the coffin appeared in the basement, it would go to a special area where all of the stuff on the outside was removed. It was always made of cheap, chrome-like plastic. That included the crosses and handles. After this was done, it was ready for the actual cremation.

A dirt burial, on the other hand, was just that — a cemetery, with plots and rows, just like any other cemetery you have ever been in. Most of the cemeteries that we dealt with were huge.

This became a problem when you had to carry the casket for 100 yards (as was the case with "The Big Deceased" person in another story).

Usually, we would arrive first at the gravesite, followed by the mourning coach, which contained the funeral director and the immediate family. On one occasion, just as I reached in to pull the casket out, the entire back piece of the casket ripped off in my hands. These things were made of really cheap materials most of the time.

The casket itself was generally made from particle board. This was a building material that was made from sawdust and wood chips, smothered in glue, and then pressed together into sheets, which were then cut up into whatever lengths you needed.

That was the case on this day. The end piece was a piece of chipboard covered with a vinyl veneer to resemble real wood. When I glanced down, I was confronted with a pair of bare feet staring at me from the end of the coffin. I freaked out because the coach had stopped, and the family was starting to get out. I yelled to Neville for guidance, and he told me that there was a small hammer in the corner of the hearse for this purpose. He said I should quickly pound the thing back on as best as I could and leave it at that. It didn't even have real nails in it. They were more like staples than anything else.

But I nailed it back on, and it held.

I had to wonder: *Whatever happened to the old guy's shoes?*

A Maltese Falcon

*T*here is an entire technique to dressing a dead person. It requires two people, a lot of skill, and some good luck. Neville and I had to dress the "clients" from time to time. Tobin Brothers had an entire department that used to handle this sort of thing, but they would occasionally get overwhelmed — or, so they said — and we would have to be pressed into service. Neither of us enjoyed doing this task, but, as with any job, when the boss tells you to do something, you usually do it, unless you are Johnny Paycheck or have a death wish of some sort.

We were sent to one of our other locations to dress a young man from Malta. This was a very sad affair. The family was completely torn up over his death. When Neville checked the clipboard, he started cursing again. He had a habit of doing this, but I found out afterwards that it was for generally good reasons. I asked him what was wrong.

He told me that this guy was at the coroner's and that they had done an autopsy on him. Of course, I didn't appreciate the significance of this until we actually got on site and saw what we had to deal with.

The family had provided all of the clothes, and they hadn't spared any cost. We started out with silk underpants and socks. Then we proceeded into silk shirts, a black bow tie and, finally, a cream-colored tuxedo. We were looking at a thousand dollars worth of apparel here.

The problem was the autopsy. He had died of an overdose, but, for some unexplained reason, they had cut into his brain. Neville said he couldn't understand that, because he had seen numerous overdose deaths.

We had to stop a blood-tinged fluid from running down his neck and onto the collar of the silk shirt, which was pure white. The incision was right in the back of this poor guy's head. We spent an hour trying to rectify the situation.

As soon as we had finished the task, they came in and announced that he had to go out immediately for the viewing. The entire family was out there, weeping and wailing. We knew that, if a single drop leaked out onto that white silk shirt, we were doomed.

Our improvised patchwork held long enough for the director to close the coffin, but it was really close.

My only suggestion to any family who find themselves in a similar situation would be to provide red clothing if your loved one has had an autopsy.

Mourning at the Grave

*Y*ou are, undoubtedly, familiar with the concept of "Urban Legends." Well, I am not sure if I started one or not.

Just think back to when we were kids. Everyone had a friend who was prepared to swear by the unequivocal truth to an eerie tale his brother's friend's uncle had related to him. Allow me to explain what happened, and I will let you be the judge as to whether or not an Urban Legend was formed.

My father had contracts with several cemeteries. We would dig their graves for them with one of our backhoes. There was one particular graveyard that was notorious for waiting to call us until the morning of needing a grave dug. St. Mary's would be frantic on the phone: "Please send someone down and dig a grave. It's all staked out, and the funeral is at 9:00 a.m.!"

My dad woke me up at 6:00 am and asked me to take the machine and "rubber" down to

St. Mary's to dig their grave. Naturally, I would start bitching about waking me up just to climb aboard a stinky backhoe at 6:30 in the morning, but my dad was not the kind of person you pushed the envelope with, so I went.

Upon arriving at the cemetery, I noticed that there was one of those strange ground fogs; it extended up about five feet from the earth. I proceeded to "hog out" the grave (backhoe-talk for "dig") and then pulled the machine over to the side and parked it.

The morning was so nice that I decided to turn off the machine and jump down into the hole, which was about six feet deep, to square off the corners. This was a routine service that we provided for the vault guys, who would arrive at 8:45 a.m.

The main road cut right down the center of the graveyard, and I was about 20 feet from it. As I scraped away in the grave, I heard voices. There were three kids coming down off the mountain, and they were cutting through the graveyard, right down the main road.

I got down in the grave and waited. You could tell they were nervous by the amount of chatter coming from them — all three talking at the same time. When they came alongside my position, I slowly started groaning and raising my gloved hand above the edge of the grave.

Keep in mind the ground fog, which just added an extra dimension to the effect.

When these kids saw that, they bolted down the road. One of them had a huge cast-iron frying pan slung from a web belt. I swear that thing was sticking straight out as the boy ran.

I started laughing so hard that I stumbled and fell back into the grave, smacking my head on the shovel.

As I drove back to the shop, the thought occurred to me that, if those boys returned later that day, there would be a brand-new grave where they would swear this thing had happened.

So, you tell *me*. Did I start an "Urban Legend" in lower Plymouth, Pennsylvania?

A Tacklebox Tragedy

My mother once told me that, if I had two really great friends when I reached the age of 60, I would be fortunate. When I finally reached that age, I found out that she was correct.

Rick Shaw was one of those friends.

We'd met in 1972 while studying at Florida Atlantic University and immediately hit it off. Rick had one of those typical Southern, laid-back personalities, having been born and raised in Oak Ridge, Tennessee. He and I kept in touch right up to the day he died at a young age from some heart-related malady. He was a picker-and-a-grinner, playing guitar and banjo, and singing throughout South Florida and, at one time, in Memphis and Nashville.

Besides all of the regular stuff that good friends get into, Rick and I liked to go fishing. During the season, we would be out on the drift boats, fishing the Gulf Stream. Usually on the *Two Georges*, an old wooden boat that had gone down navigating the Boynton Inlet and was raised to be placed back into service.

At one time we went halvies on a "Johnboat," which we used in the canals around his house in Lakeworth. The only problem was that the state of Florida issued an advisory about the excessive mercury content of the fish caught in those canals, which meant that we were forced to catch and release, something that Rick and I rarely did. We fished for food. One day, we went down to the Boynton Inlet to do some surf-casting from the jetty. All of the old black guys were close to shore and not bunched up on the end of the jetty as they usually were, so we saw this as a golden opportunity to possibly land some Jacks.

Rick and I made our way out to the end of the jetty and noticed that the old black guys were just smiling. No one said a word to us, but they all just smiled as we passed. We were both carrying two rod-and-reels, plus our tackleboxes.

We got out to the end and put our tackleboxes down while we prepared our hooks with a few artificial lures, when suddenly a huge wave broke over the jetty. If it hadn't been for the cable railings, we both would have been swept out to sea, but we watched in horror as our extra rods and tackleboxes were swept away — simply washed from existence in one fell swoop.

This pretty much ended my sport-fishing career in Florida for all time. If you know anything about an old and trusted tacklebox, you would appreciate this sentiment. It would be hard to replace, to say the least.

Then we realized why the old guys had been smiling. They knew what was going to happen out there at the end of the jetty.

Tony's Cadillac

*P*rior to being shipped off to Vietnam, I was stationed at the Philadelphia Naval Shipyard in Philadelphia, Pennsylvania. This location was approximately 110 miles from where my parents' house was, and this made it possible to go home on weekends. I did this for several weeks by using the bus, which presented its own set of hassles, as the bus station was downtown, and the shipyard was on the South side of the city.

One Sunday night after I returned from Wilkes-Barre, I was walking through the bus station on my way to Broad Street, where I could catch a local to the shipyard, when I encountered a gentleman in the shadows. He started walking alongside me and asking if I wanted to "…buy something that would keep me warm all night."

The guy kept walking, keeping pace with me and asking the same question: "Do you wanna' buy something that will keep you warm all night?" Finally, we came upon an area where, behind a concrete pylon, he had a large cardboard box. In it were the cheapest-looking electric blankets that I had ever seen.

Eventually, I made a few friends on the base, and one of those was a guy named Tony. He owned a huge black Cadillac. We found three other guys from the Wilkes-Barre area and formed a carpool. Tony was going home every weekend, anyway — why not make a few dollars in the process?

So. we all chipped in and got a comfortable ride directly from the Naval Shipyard to our hometown — right from the main gate, up and back. This meant that I wouldn't have to walk through the bus station anymore.

After our stay, we would all meet at Andy's diner for the return trip. One Sunday night, we decided to buy a case of beer for the return journey. You must bear in mind that, back then, the drinking-and-driving laws were a bit less harsh. So a couple of beers each would soften the drive back.

Everything was going smoothly. We were on the Pennsylvania Turnpike, cruising in our big black Cadillac, when someone — I think it was Angelo — started saying that he had to take a piss. Tony was in no mood to stop at that time, so Angie just had to hold it until Tony had to relieve himself, also.

We had passed the Howard Johnson's, so there weren't any more pit stops on that road until we hit the Surekill (aka "Schuylkill") Expressway. The number of voices increased to the point where Tony just wheeled his Caddy onto the shoulder and stopped. He told us that this was as good as it was going to get.

There we were, five sailors dressed in our dress-blue uniforms, lined up against the side of a black Cadillac, having a pissing contest alongside the road on the Pennsylvania Turnpike. Cars were whizzing by, honking their horns, and we just said nasty things in Italian and kept on pissing. Eventually, a car slowed down and stopped behind us. They left their headlights on, and it illuminated these five streams of golden liquid all trying to piss over the snow bank.

As it turned out, the driver of the car was a Pennsylvania State Trooper.

I don't know if you have ever been stopped on the Pennsylvania Turnpike by a State Trooper. It is a frightening experience, to say the least. For years, it was their policy to not hire anyone who was less than 7 feet tall. They all wore those "campaign" hats, which just added to the image.

Well, as it turned out, this particular State Trooper happened to be one of the few women that they had on the force, and she was not happy.

Our dress-blue uniform trousers came with the infamous 13 buttons. It required great dexterity, even on a good day, to close the front of those bell-bottoms, and here we were, half in the bag, trying to accomplish this feat,

This woman read us the riot act and threatened to haul us off to the local drunk tank. She wanted to know why we were desecrating her highway with urine and, more importantly, why we were engaged in this nefarious act standing on the side of HER roadway.

It looked really bad for a while until Angelo piped up. Angelo was one of those little Italian guys with an angelic face. He prided himself on being a real ladies' man and had the lines down pat to prove it. Angelo started to explain that we had all been ordered to Vietnam and that this was our last night out before being shipped out. He really poured it on until she finally capitulated and let us go with the warning that, next time, there wouldn't be any mercy.

The trouble was that I hadn't yet told the guys that I actually did have orders to ship out to Vietnam.

Within a week, I was gone.

Young Man and the Sea

*E*rnest Hemingway loved to fish off of the island of Cuba.

He was renowned for his capabilities as a deep-sea fisherman, going after the big boys, usually Marlin. Rick Shaw and I may have dreamed of landing a big fish, but we had to contend with Kingfish, Wahoo, and on occasion, Bonita.

The *Two Georges* was a drift boat out of Delray Beach, Florida. It had sunk once navigating the Boynton Inlet, and they'd raised it for more service as a fishing boat. The old-timers swore that it made a difference having a wooden boat under you. They claimed that the steel-hulled boats made too much noise, and that, in turn, chased the fish away. I can't comment on that either way. All I know is that the *Two Georges* had a liberal policy when it came to alcoholic beverages, and we always took advantage of that.

One of the advantages of drift fishing in Florida was the proximity of the Gulf Stream — only one mile off the coast of Palm Beach County. The Gulf Stream provided us with extremely good prospects when it came to catching fish. We found that the early-morning and the evening excursions were the best. It seemed that the fish were not very active during the course of the middle part of the day. The early trip left the dock at about 7:00 a.m. and made it to the fishing area in around 20 minutes.

With drift fishing, you may have 15 people standing along one rail with short rods loaded with 50-lb.-test line. The object was to drift along and have all of the lines being pulled by the boat. The mates would bait your hooks for you, but, as you became more experienced, you learned to do that yourself because it sometimes took too much time for them to get to you. We used Mackerel bait fish; they were really oily, which attracted more fish.

On the trip out to the Gulf Stream, a "pool" would be formed. You gave one person $2 and joined the pool. Usually, the rules were quite simple: The largest fish brought onboard would win the pool. As fish were caught, the mates would mark them with their knives. They would put two slashes on the head, for example, to designate your catch — two strikes on the head, or cut tail, that sort of thing.

One morning, we were out there on the water. The pool was pretty high, because they decided to up the bet to $3 per person, and there were about 20 people on board. Rick and I were positioned up by the bow of the boat, and standing next to us was an obnoxious guy from New Jersey. He was loud and kept shouting out things that were outrageous.

We figured that he still had a buzz on from the night before. This was one of the drawbacks to fishing during the height of the tourist season. At 7:00 a.m., no one was in the mood for loud, obnoxious people from any state of the union, let alone New Jersey. This guy kept bragging about how he was going to win the pool and that we were a bunch of suckers for even trying.

We knew the skipper, and you could see by his facial expression that this clown was getting on his nerves. You must understand that the *Two Georges* was a bit of a pirate boat in the industry, with all of the drinking and its infamous history of having been pulled off the bottom.

So, there we were, fishing away in the early-morning hours, with a pool worth $60. That would have paid for our fare and our beer in one fell swoop.

We ran into a school of Kingfish, and the action got pretty hectic. Kingfish are in the

Mackerel family and look like a fancy Barracuda. You can eat them, but they're gamey, with a very strong flavor. I would cook them up with a beer batter and have them for dinner only once or twice during the season. I liked to fish the bottom for Grouper myself, because Rick and I went out there to catch food fish. If we snagged a big Kingfish and won the pool, well, that was a bonus.

This obnoxious guy hooked a big Kingfish and started reeling it in. All the while, he was shouting out about winning the pool: *"Just like I told you dopes, I am going to win that pool!"*

Now you must understand that Kingfish sometimes would travel in pairs, and when you hooked one, the other would follow that fish right up to the surface. So Rick and I both noticed this silver streak following the Kingfish on this guy's line, and we thought it was the other fish. Just as the mate gaffed the fish and was starting to pull it aboard the boat, a large shark came right out of the water. In an instant, only half of the Kingfish was still on the hook, and this had been a really big fish.

The skipper leaned out of the bridge, spat some tobacco juice, and said, "It has to be a *whole fish* to win the pool!"

Flight of the Valkyries

Briny Breezes was a small swath of land that jutted out into the Atlantic Ocean in a town called Boynton Beach, Florida.

It was the only trailer park located on the ocean in all of South Florida. Adjacent to Briny Breezes was a parcel of land that was no more than 500 yards wide. It was populated with one-story buildings and had its own beach access. This little enclave was my home for more than five years.

I rented a small beach house from a Canadian couple. From the front door, I could see the ocean and could hear the waves crashing at night. It was a quaint setting, conducive to the old beachcomber mentality.

My range hood quit working one day, so I had an electrician friend of mine come and take a look at it. The thing was wired on a 220-amp line, which struck him as being rather queer, given that the device needed only half that amount of power to operate. We followed the wire out of the house and over to the back of their sons' surf shop. As it turned out, I'd been paying to run a 15,000-BTU air conditioner for more than five years.

When I brought this to the landlord's attention, he duly evicted me.

But they had made one fatal mistake.

One night, while under the influence of copious amounts of bourbon, they'd admitted to me that they'd never received U.S. citizenship. Being the patriotic American that I think I am, I immediately brought this to the attention of the INS, who promptly deported them back to Canada. You could say that it turned out to be a very expensive air conditioner to operate.

But that is not really what I set out here to tell you about — or should I say, *"aboot,"* as the Canadians would pronounce it.

I wanted to tell you a little story that had a horrible outcome.

Approximately a half-mile from my beach house was the Intercoastal Waterway, and just north of where I lived, there was a drawbridge over that famous stretch of water. Right next to the drawbridge, there was a trendy little restaurant with one of those trendy little names like Andrew's, or maybe even Trevor's. It really doesn't matter — it's probably something else by now, anyway.

This place had a nice deck overlooking the Intercoastal Waterway and also had docking provisions for all of the rich drug dealers in their cigarette boats. I used to frequent this place on a regular basis, sitting out, drinking tall alcoholic drinks, and occasionally having a fried-fish sandwich.

When you spend a lot of time in Florida, especially near the beach, you will notice the behavior of the pelicans that always fly by each day. In the morning, they fly South to their fishing grounds, and then, later that day, they come back North to roost, full of delicious fish. You may also notice that they have a particular way of relieving themselves when flying. They sort of rear up and extend their bottoms out in front and let loose with a white, sticky substance.

I was sitting there at the restaurant one afternoon, just relaxing and reminding myself why I lived in South Florida. Right across from me sat an older couple, a man and wife, smartly dressed and waiting for their dinners to arrive.

It was about 6:00 p.m., and the sky was simply beautiful, a perfect Florida evening. Finally the couple's dinner arrived, and it was a rather generous one — fish, with a couple of side dishes. They were just starting in on it when a flock of pelicans came by, flying North as they usually do at this time of day.

I noticed one starting to rear up in a typical pelican-pooping sort of way and braced myself for impact. I actually felt the moisture of this load pass by my right ear, it was that close. Then it just laid itself right across the lady's dinner, up onto her chest, and ended on her forehead. This white goo of semi-digested fish products just pasted her hair to her head.

They just sat there for a few seconds in shock. The husband tried to wipe some of this stuff off of his wife's face with a paper napkin, without much success. Then, they just stood up and walked out.

Allow me to venture this suggestion: Be very mindful of the pelicans' flight path when visiting South Florida to avoid a confrontation with pelican bathroom manners.

Being American in Dublin

*N*ormally, we fly direct from either Philadelphia or Newark straight through to Dublin. Every year, we spend a week both coming and going in Dublin. It's a great town.

One of my many pleasures is staying at the Central Hotel in Exchequer Street — a perfect location for enjoying most of what Dublin has to offer. The Central is located right at the bottom of Grafton Street, a world-renowned shopping and entertainment district. It is also a great place to just walk and take it all in — from street performances, to music, to mimes. There are people who cover themselves in a grey metallic coating of some sort and then stand perfectly still for what seems like hours.

One day, a pigeon was perched on the pipe sticking out of the mouth of what appeared to be a statue of the poet and novelist James Joyce. It looked so real that I was convinced that the statue was just that — a statue cast in metal. The illusion stood for several minutes, until I noticed an eye blink. It was only then that I realized that it was a real, live person standing there for my benefit. Tipping him became a necessity.

Some of the best restaurants in Dublin are located within a few blocks of The Central, and the hotel maintains one of the best-kept secrets in town, The Library Bar. It's a pub located on the second floor that features a couple of real fireplaces that are kept burning throughout the Winter months. There are easy chairs and couches for seating, and, of course, it is all surrounded with bookshelves.

When I'm not in The Library Bar, I like to walk down Exchequer Street and browse in "The Secret Bookstore" or sit at a sidewalk table at Butler's Coffee Shop, right on the corner of Williams Street. Butler's gives you a piece of homemade chocolate with every cup of coffee that you purchase, and they have a "frequent-flyer" program: Ten cups warrants a free one. Plus, it's just a great place to sit and watch Dublin walk by. As I mentioned, it's a great city, populated with very young people. I would say that the average age in Dublin is somewhere between 25 and 30.

One afternoon, I was standing in Butler's, waiting for my Americano with milk. As with most busy coffee shops, they have part of the counter set aside for picking up orders. There isn't any table service at Butlers. You place your order, wait until it's ready, pick it up, and sit wherever you choose.

On this particular day, as I stood there, I noticed two gentlemen talking. One of them was leaning on that portion of the counter set aside for pickups. Finally, I couldn't take it any longer, and I said to the guy, "Hey, pal, you're standing in the pickup area." With that, he glanced around and said, "Well, it can't be much of an emergency — there's nothing to be picked up."

It was then that I realized my "Americanism." He was absolutely correct in his observation that there wasn't anything to be picked up. But, I, being thoroughly indoctrinated in the ways of single file and the sanctity of the pickup counter, stood corrected.

In short, I was an American living in Dublin.

Navy Tradition

*S*peaking from my own personal experience, I can attest to the fact that the United States Navy is based on many old traditions.

In 1968, when I enlisted in the Navy, I was sent to boot camp at their facility at Great Lakes, Michigan. While there, we had to wash our own clothes and put them on a clothesline, but we didn't use regular clothespins like any normal person. We used short lengths of rope, and everything had to be tied onto the line. Plus, all of the bows had to be in perfect order, or else the instructor would untie them and let the clothing drop onto the ground.

Another practice was the use of "blanket parties." I was stationed aboard an old tub called an "LST." That acronym stood for "Long Slow Target" in the vernacular of the ordinary sailor. But, officially, the Navy called it a Landing Ship Tank. This particular bucket of bolts had been built for the assault on Okinawa during The

Second World War, and it was a piece of junk. We had to sail that beast across the Pacific Ocean from Vietnam to Long Beach, California.

While at sea, we had a machinist's mate who worked in the boiler room. He wasn't the sharpest pencil in the box and was one of those really irritating type of people who was always telling tall tales. As they say in the Navy — please pardon the expression — if a story starts with the word "No shit!" it is probably a lie.

This guy was on duty one night and forgot to close the seacocks. They were valves that allowed seawater into certain tanks to stabilize the ship. Well, he fell asleep and forgot to turn the things off. The cold seawater came very close to hitting the red-hot steam boilers, which would have blown a hole in the bottom of the ship that you could have driven a car through.

Later that evening, he got a "blanket party." I know this for a fact because I was one of the people who participated.

A "blanket party" is pretty simple. People would lie in ambush, and, when you were least expecting it, a blanket would be thrown over your head, and everyone present would beat the crap out of you. The reason for the blanket was to protect the identities of the perpetrators of the dastardly deed.

Another tradition was called the "Red Alert." Setting up a Red Alert required great care. With a person sleeping in his bunk, we would very carefully pull a sheet over that person's face. Then, ever so gently, another guy would squat down right over the victim's face with their ass just above that individual. Naturally, the squatter didn't have any underwear on. At the signal, everyone would shout, "Red Alert, Red Alert," and the sheet would be pulled down as the victim jerked his head up, placing his nose into a place where the sun never shines.

It sounds disgusting, doesn't it? Well, it is — very disgusting. But if it is done right, the word will get around to the entire fleet, and the people who pull it off are heroes for a day.

I won't address the poor fellow who provided the face.

A Failure to Communicate

My friend Charles owned a large automobile dealership in Kingston, Pennsylvania. If I am not mistaken, his father was the first person in the state to import the Volkswagen Beetle back in the 1950s. Charles sold Volkswagens, Porsches, and, as he would say, the Mazdas that paid the light bill.

Charles decided to build a new dealership next to his existing one and sell Lincoln Mercuries. The problem was, a very deep ravine was located where his dealership was to go. My father's trucks were hired to transport a huge amount of dirt from across the river and onto this building site. We worked on that job for months, because it was a big project. The lot was about the size of two football fields, and it was about 140 feet deep. Every foot had to be put down and compacted before the next foot could be added.

The material would be brought in, a bulldozer would spread the dirt, and then a series of compacting machines would pound it into a hard surface before going on to the next "lift," as they were called. Each lift had to be tested for compaction before being approved by the building inspectors.

Jackie, another friend of ours, was the bulldozer operator. He ran a D8 Caterpillar. This machine was huge. It had big tracks and was the size of a small house. When you operate a machine of that size, you learn not to look behind you when it's in reverse. The blade in the front could move close to 20 tons of dirt in one fell swoop. You would back up to a certain point, drop the massive blade, and then pull forward, spreading the dirt in an even 18-inch layer. Then the other machines would come in behind you and pound the dirt into a very hard surface. If the compaction wasn't right, any buildings that were built on the lot would eventually sink into the ground.

There was a young guy who came in a few times a day to take readings with a special device that measured the compaction level of the dirt. It would shoot a sound wave into the earth and then figure out how hard the soil was. If it failed, they would have to beat on the ground some more and then re-test it.

Nobody much cared for this young guy

because he was actually over-doing his job. He would demand perfection in areas that were way too big for nitpicking. Another thing that the other guys didn't like was the way he would drive right up to the area that needed testing and park his car. He was too lazy to carry his device any distance.

Over the course of the job, we all tried to tell this guy to be very careful. We tried to explain that D8 Caterpillar operators didn't look behind them when they were backing up. They didn't have to, because there wasn't supposed to be anything there.

Well, one day, the inevitable happened. The inspector drove his car onto the lot and parked it right behind Jackie's bulldozer. When he reversed, he backed right over the guy's car and squashed it into the ground. I don't think that Jackie's boss paid for the car, either. It was well known that everyone had repeatedly tried to warn him not to park his car behind the bulldozer. The young guy failed to understand the consequence of his actions until it was too late.

Jason Goodman

Key West Burning

*W*hile living in Key West, Florida, I worked for two different companies, operating heavy equipment. The first was a firm called Toppino's, Inc. They had the contract to haul material up to "Mount Trashmore."

Now, Key West did have a trash incinerator at one time. The state of Florida went to great expense installing this brand-new facility. They also had a new desalination plant, but these two technologically advanced entities were rendered useless by an old, standing custom in the Keys called "The Bubba System." How this worked was quite simple: Once certain individuals got into office, they would hire all of their relatives to operate these high-tech devices, with the result that the devices were completely useless after a relatively short period of time.

The consequences of these actions were twofold: One, they had to import all of the fresh drinking water from Miami at great expense.

Trust me — I am not exaggerating when I say "great expense." Key West was the only place I have ever lived where I was conscious of the cost when I flushed the toilet. The second problem associated with The Bubba System was, as I mentioned, the fact that Toppino's, Inc. had the contract to carry dirt to the top of "Mount Trashmore."

"Mount Trashmore" was the local name for the huge pile of trash that was located on Stock Island. You can see it quite clearly when driving down US 1, the main road both into and out of the city. This thing had to be at least 500 feet high — a giant mountain of trash covered with a white dirt called "Marl."

Whenever a developer wanted to sell waterfront property in Florida, they would hire the companies that I worked for to dig really deep lakes. This was how they raised the building lots above the floodplain. These lakes refilled with brackish water as quickly as we could dig them. They would use a machine called a "drag line" to scoop the wet material out of the earth, and then we would load it into trucks and deposit it on top of Mount Trashmore.

Another contract that I worked on was the Coast Guard Station located in downtown Key West. While putzing around with my backhoe,

I would see large piles of marijuana stacked in bales on the dock.

Next to the dock would be boats. Sometimes they would show the telltale marks of a .50-caliber machine gun — probably as a result of the owners of said boats refusing to stop for a Coast Guard vessel. You could call that "governmental persuasion."

Usually, there would be armed guards standing around these heaps of marijuana, just to make sure that it wasn't recycled into the food chain. After a certain period of time, they would load all of these bales into a warehouse in some undisclosed location. When the undisclosed location became too full, they would remove the marijuana to another undisclosed location somewhere in Miami.

Well, one day, the powers-that-be, in their glorious "Bubba" wisdom, decided that it was too much trouble carting large quantities of marijuana around the state. So, they decided to take a few truckloads to the top of Mount Trashmore and burn it.

The plan seemed quite sound on paper: Pile up the bales into a stack about 50 feet x 50 feet x 50 feet and set fire to it with flame throwers. All was going according to plan until they realized that a condensed stack like that wouldn't necessarily burn, *per se,* as much as smolder, which was acceptable until the wind changed direction.

Keep in mind that Key West is an island stuck out into the Atlantic Ocean and is prone to various winds coming in from different directions. The wind changed direction over that entire weekend and blew over the city of Key West. Huge clouds of premium marijuana smoke wafted lazily across the city. The entire town was getting high whether they wanted to or not. Their solution was to bring up the fire trucks and pour copious amounts of water onto the blaze, which just made it smoke all the more, increasing the citywide high in Key West for that long weekend.

I would imagine that there was a run on snack foods in town for a few days, coupled with a substantial amount of laughter.

Scratching and Pointing

In Boulder, Colorado, I worked again as a heavy equipment operator. I was employed by a company named Boulder Excavators and enjoyed a very fulfilling experience.

This company would always have me "rubber" my machine to any given job. To "rubber" a machine meant that you drive it from job to job, as opposed to placing it on a trailer and hauling it there. One day, I was rubbering up to the tree line — that's 12,000 feet up, by the way — smoking a doobie and realizing that I was making a lot of money every hour for the privilege of being able to work there.

Broadway was the main artery that ran out of the city East to West. If you stayed on it, you would end up in Longmont, Colorado.

Right in town on a corner was a popular bar named "Potter's." I used to drink there because it was a great place for a boy to meet a girl. One night, I was standing at the bar, chatting up a young sweet thing, when she got around to asking me what I did for a living.

I didn't go into detail about rubbering a machine and smoking pot in the process, but I did explain my work. I told her that I was a heavy-equipment operator and explained what that entailed. She was pensive for a moment, thinking, and then she came back with this little piece of observational wisdom. She said, "What is it with you guys? Every time I see a construction site, all of you are standing around, pointing at the ground, and scratching your balls ....."

The more I thought about that description, the more sense it made. I'd spent a great deal of my life around those same construction sites, and she was absolutely correct.

From that moment on, I would take note of what everyone was doing on the typical construction site. Sure enough, we were scratching our balls and pointing at a hole in the ground.

Jazz on the East Side

Wilkes-Barre, Pennsylvania, is a dirty, little, depressing, and disgusting town.

The "dirty" part comes from the fact that it is an old coal town. Everything is covered with a coating of grey dust that comes from the slag heaps still evident around the valley.

The "depressing" part derives from the political hacks that run the place. You could say that they were not interested in the cultural welfare of their constituents. They pretty much confine themselves to lining their pockets with the money that is supposed to pull everyone up and out of the quagmire of ignorance and poverty.

And the "disgusting" part comes from the numerous scandals that plague Wilkes-Barre, from the "kids for cash" debacle to the pornography rings that specialize in abuse.

Man, what a brilliant legacy.

Another fact about this town is that it's boring. Let me just put it this way: You will not find too many bottles of Rothschild '36 in the liquor stores there, and the only champagne is either Andre or Chateau Lucerne, the stuff that you cover with a piece of tin foil and it still has bubbles after a week.

Anyway, I bought a 1956 Ford Thunderbird from a student at Kings University. These were classic Ford automobiles, and the one that I got had a standard shift right from the factory, which made it even more desirable. I restored the thing to close-to-showroom condition and used it to escape on weekends. One addition I did make was to install an 8-Track cassette system, which allowed me versatility when it came to music.

One night, I was drinking in a cocktail lounge called Vispi's. The place was owned by a gay guy and attracted gentlemen of the same persuasion. The women really appreciated this fact because they didn't feel threatened in a gay place, because, normally, gay guys don't hit on straight women.

But I did. That was why I used to hang out there. My macho friends thought that I may be slipping into the abyss by hanging out at Vispi's, but I never felt any need to tell them about the ladies there.

On one particular night, it was a bit slow, so I decided to drive down to New York City for some entertainment. The trip normally took about two hours, and this is where my cassette deck came into play. I had just bought Dave Brubeck's *Take Five* album. So I popped it into the player and just let it play. One of the nice things about the old 8-Tracks was that, if you didn't eject the tape, it would play until it self-destructed.

I found this nice little bar on the East Side. Lo and behold — guess who was playing? The George Shearing Trio, another of my favorite jazz groups. So I parked myself at the bar and just took in the sound. It was great.

After a few minutes, a guy walked in and sat not too far from me at the bar. Between numbers, we struck up a conversation about jazz in general and other current events, but mostly about the music. I went into great detail about the new Dave Brubeck album that I had listened to on my trip down to the city.

After about 45 minutes, the guy told me he had to go and bid me farewell. He walked over and spoke to George Shearing for a few minutes and then exited the place. I went back to my listening and drinking enjoyment.

When it came time to refresh my drink, the bartender told me that the gentleman I had been talking to had bought this round. So, I started chatting with the bartender about some of our conversation — the drive down from Wilkes-

Barre, listening to the Dave Brubeck Quartet on the tape player, how great the *Take Five* album sounded.

The bartender stopped me and asked, "Didn't you know who you were talking to just now?"

I said, "No" — that I didn't have a clue as to who the guy was.

The bartender, in typical New York understatement, said, "Buddy, that was Dave Brubeck."

Moscow in Manhattan

My first wife's parents were divorced. They had both remarried, and both lived in New York. Her father was a famous doctor and lived on Park Avenue in Manhattan. Her mother became a multi-millionaire and lived in Stony Brook, Palm Beach, and Lyons, France.

It was always interesting visiting her mother on Long Island. She and her husband would go out on a Saturday and buy all kinds of antiques. Then, on Friday night, after a session at Mario's, they would come home, have a heated argument, and smash all of the antiques in the house. They used them as projectiles, something akin to very old, musty hand grenades. The pattern would repeat itself every weekend.

Park Avenue was another story entirely. The good doctor would start drinking bourbon early, and, somewhere between the soup and salad courses, he would accuse me of all kinds of foul deeds committed upon the person known as his daughter. It was at this point that I would make my escape out into the night in downtown Manhattan.

My wife had a younger brother, named Russell. Sometimes, he would be in town for the holidays, and we would go out together just to enjoy New York City. On Lexington Avenue, right around the corner from the doctor's building, there used to be a bar called "The Wiffenpoof" — I kid you not; that was the name of the place.

Now, it could have been a gay bar, and with a name like "The Wiffenpoof," it wouldn't require   too much imagination to arrive at that conclusion. But the reason we were attracted to the place was its ale. They had Watney's Red Barrel Ale on tap at The Wiffenpoof. Watney's is an old English ale, and, in the glass, it takes on a red color — hence, "Red Barrel." Our code was to walk around the corner to The Wiffenpoof and "…quaff a few Watneys." You had to use a really poor English accent when you said this, as in, *"I say, Jason, let us pop over and quaff a few Watneys — 'ey whot?"*

One evening, we did just that. There we were, seated comfortably at the bar with a few cold Watneys in front of us, telling stories of debauchery and pillage, when in walked Nikita Sergeyevich Khrushchev.

I was shocked. I thought that he had mysteriously disappeared while sunning himself at his dacha outside Moscow. But here he was, at The Wiffenpoof on Lexington Avenue in New York City. Then again, by this time, I had spent enough time in New York City to realize that anything could happen there — and usually did. Over the years, I had seen any number of famous people in New York, and, of course, New Yorkers are so cool, they just totally ignore them.

But, still, it was hard to ignore *Nikita Khrushchev.* I took special note that he was wearing both of his shoes.

Anything *could* happen that night at The Wiffenpoof.

Mr. Khrushchev had taken up a position next to Russell, and I couldn't help but stare. The guy was perfect — right down to the mole on the side of his face.

But Nikita spoke with a definite Bronx accent.

He used the "turdy-turd and turd" ("Thirty-third and Third") lingo of a lifelong "New Yawk" resident.

So, after a few minutes, I couldn't take it anymore.

I leaned over and said, "Hey, Nikita. I thought you had accidentally shot yourself in the back of the head. What are you doing here in New York?"

He explained that his name was "Bernie" and that he had made his money as Nikita Khrushchev's double when he was in power in Russia but, now, he rarely got called.

Anyway, we proceeded to talk about a myriad of subjects, and the Watneys kept flowing. They started to go down easily, which should have been a warning. I noticed that Russell had started to look uncomfortable. He was sort of squirming around on his stool. So, I asked him if anything was wrong. He told me that Mr. Khrushchev had his hand on his thigh and was whispering sweet things into his right ear.

Russell asked me for help, and I was rendered powerless. The thought of Nikita Khrushchev feeling up my brother-in-law and friend Russell in a New York bar was entirely too outrageous to grasp.

The $8000 Bra

*M*ort Miller was the Supervisor of Maintenance for the Wyoming Valley School District.

He had also worked for our father years previous, which pretty much guaranteed that we would be called when work had to be done around the many school buildings.

One day, Mort called with a real problem. The entire sewer system at Plymouth High School had backed up. This was quite serious — they had to cancel all classes at the old building. Goodman and Sons Excavating got the call. My brother Mark and I made up two of the "Sons."

Mort decided that we should start at the street and make our way toward the school until we ran into the old terra cotta sewer line. This way, we could replace much of the line with more modern materials and, hopefully, stave off another crisis along this line.

We had to cut the street in front of the school

using concrete saws and a jackhammer. So, we started at the nearest manhole and laid out a straight line toward the school. After we opened the street, I was the unfortunate volunteer who had to go down into the manhole.

As it turned out, when they'd installed the new manholes and sewer lines in the streets a few years earlier, they emptied the remains of a concrete truck alongside the manhole that we had to work from. There was more than three feet of concrete that we had to jackhammer a hole through to accommodate an eight-inch plastic sewer line.

I was positioned eight feet below the surface of the street inside the manhole. My feet were straddling the running water and other delights that ran through. My jackhammer was suspended on a chain, so that I could beat on this concrete plug. Every day for five days, I would climb down this short piece of ladder. Then my brother would pull the ladder up and out until lunchtime. I did this the entire week. At 8:00 a.m., I would enter the manhole, bust concrete until noon, emerge for lunch, and then return to my office underground until 4:00 p.m.

It was a difficult job. I had to wear ear protection, a dust mask, overalls, and huge black rubber boots. It must have been a sight when I climbed up out of the street all suited up for destruction.

The job was nasty and dirty; the smell was far from enticing.

But a few quirks did arise. About two blocks up the street was the site of the Hershey Ice Cream Company. Every day at 9:00 a.m., the manhole would fill with the smell of vanilla. When I looked down, I could see white water between my boots. Then, at 3:00 p.m., the place would fill with the smell of chocolate, and the water would assume that color. This was just one of those little details that I could relate at the bar after work, over a few beers.

My brother Mark was situated in a hole next to the manhole I was in with another jackhammer.

We were attacking this problem from both sides, and the going was really hard. The concrete that had been inadvertently poured alongside the manhole was called "High Early."

This was a particular mix of concrete that was especially hard. It had additional "Portland" cement in it for that purpose. It was used under the blacktop of the street to keep the surface from settling into a pothole.

This was our demise. "High Early" does not fall off in large chunks when you strike it with a jackhammer. It comes off in little chips — almost flakes. We had to work hard for every inch we cut into that stuff. Hence, the entire week was spent just busting a hole through the side of this manhole.

Finally, we'd done it — a nice hole that would accept an eight-inch sewer pipe. After this was completed, the rest of the job went relatively smoothly. It was just a matter of digging a trench with the backhoe, laying the pipe as we went along.

After about 50 feet, my brother ran into the old pipeline from the High School. We dug on top of it, replacing the old terra cotta sections with eight-inch PVC pipe. While digging, my brother ran into a "Y" in the old pipe. This is where two lines meet and converge into just one.

Upon closer examination, we found a huge bra inside the pipe. One of the cups was perfectly inflated, you might say, and made a perfect plug for the eight-inch terra cotta sewer line.

We had found the problem — the thing that had backed up an entire high school plumbing system.

When Mort Miller stopped at the job site, we presented him this huge bra and explained that it was the reason for all of his headaches.

That bra hung on the wall in Mort's office for 15 years. It was left in the same place right up until he retired from his position with the school district. Under the bra was a small sign that read: "This is an $8000 bra."

The Demon Substitute

For one particular Halloween night, I wanted to do something really weird.

I found a little shop in West Scranton, Pennsylvania, that sold all types of theatrical supplies. I drove up there and bought some stage makeup and a can of silver hair spray. (I won't make you guess where I got that idea. Check out another story in this book called "Death of a Coiffure.")

Anyway, to complete my ensemble, I also purchased a few tabs of THC. Do you remember that? It was supposed to be the active ingredient in marijuana that came in a pill form. It didn't matter what was actually in it. The stuff gave you a nice, pleasant buzz.

Earlier that evening, I'd done my face and my neck in purple. Then I painted my lips dark blue and smeared black around my eyes. To top it all off, I sprayed my hair silver. Then I put on regular street clothes. The idea was to portray a demon of sorts and amplify the effect by being dressed normally.

Most of the cocktail lounges and bars that I would frequent offered all kinds of specials for people who came dressed in costume. My choice proved to be really effective — in fact, I was actually scaring a lot of people out of their wits. At the one place, called Vispi's, they used a red lighting scheme, which, in turn, enhanced the effect of my makeup, with the end result being a really convincing demon.

At this same time, I had just completed my Bachelor's Degree in Art Education. I had attended Florida Atlantic University and upon completion returned to Pennsylvania just to hang out and wait until another adventure presented itself.

My mother suggested that I sign up for substitute teaching. It paid well and really didn't tie me down to any kind of contractual agreement in case anything else came up. So, this is what I did. The only problem is that they would call on the morning that they needed me — not before. I'd have only about a two-hour window between the phone call and having to be at a particular school in the Wyoming Valley School District system.

I'd been out fairly late on Halloween night. With

the THC and a several well-placed cocktails, I was really flying through the whole evening, not to mention all the fun of being Beelzebub for a night.

Yep. You guessed it — they called me at 7:00 a.m. the next morning.

There I was, in the bathroom, scrubbing my face with a washcloth. The makeup wasn't coming off. I asked my mother what I could use to remove this stuff, and she said, "You mean you didn't put down a base of Noxema?"

I said, "Noxema? What Noxema? What is that?"

She went on to explain that I should have coated my face with cold cream — that way, I'd have been able to remove the stage makeup.

Hell, I didn't know anything about that, and the people at the shop where I'd bought those products probably just assumed that I knew what I was doing and didn't say a word about "Noxema."

So I proceeded to scrub some more. I even considered using steel wool on my face, but that idea was nixed in favor of having actual flesh left there. Time was running out. I had to be at the Forty-Fort Elementary School in 20 minutes, or I would lose $50, which was a lot of money back then — and money that I desperately needed to plan my big escape.

At 9:00 a.m., I walked into my first classroom. Some of the kids just stared, others screamed, and a few just thought that it was the best thing they had seen since sliced bread.

The ruckus attracted the attention of the old bags who ran the place. They stopped by my classroom and just stood there with their lower jaw on their chest. There I was — purple-faced, blue-lipped, and blackened eyes, not to mention the silver hair. I quickly became The Demon Substitute Teacher.

Needless to say, I was never called again with the opportunity to impart my immense knowledge in the realm of art.

As for the makeup, it took weeks to wear off my face.

My Mexican BLT

*Y*ears ago, my design business was going great guns.

My accountant told me that I had to "lose" some money somewhere or give it to the IRS. It was just then that my wife and I received an invitation to travel to Puerto Vallarta, Mexico, for a week's stay at the *Sol Melia* resort there. The place was so nice that I decided to buy a timeshare, and we have been going there ever since.

Sol Melia is a Spanish company that operates resorts and hotels all over the world. Their places are all first-class operations, with all of the amenities that you would expect at a top-notch resort.

One year, I decided that I was going to experience everything the place had to offer.

I started with the parasailing event on the beach, flying through the air strapped to a parachute and being towed by a high-powered speedboat.

It was fantastic — there was no noise except the wind whipping past my ears. I looked down, past my toes, to see if I could see anything. But there was only the air and the seawater, some 800 feet below.

We tried all of the restaurants because, that year, we'd bought into the all-inclusive option. Our apartment had a small kitchen, and there was a store within walking distance, but, during this particular stay, we decided to take a break from cooking, also.

My wife used the services of the spa, getting her nails done and a full facial, plus the hot mud bath — the whole nine yards of pampered luxury. While she was there, I decided to spend some time at the massage tent.

For $50, I got a 30-minute massage. The setting was absolutely stunning — a white canvas tent set up right next to the sea wall. As a young woman worked on me, I lay there, just listening to the gentle waves lap the beach. It was very relaxing, to say the least.

She had me turn over onto my back and then proceeded to work on my chest and legs. I actually started to fall into a brilliant sleep, slipping just below the surface of consciousness.

Suddenly, this little voice, close to my left ear, asked, "Do you want mayonnaise?"

Confusion reigned for a few seconds. I didn't quite catch the gist of what she meant, because I never ordered a Mexican Bacon, Lettuce, and Tomato sandwich.

Of course!

What else could it have been?

Nightmare Under the Elm Trees

*P*ennsylvania Summers are really nice, and, now, with global warming, they are becoming even better — they last a lot longer.

Not too many people had swimming pools when I was growing up. That was the domain of a select few in my neighborhood, and I didn't travel in those circles back then.

What we did have were mountain streams and water holes. I remember one such place. It was on the side of a coal strip-mine pit, where the giant shovels had thrown out some clay, and a small stream had filled the hole with water. We called the place "The Pollywog."

It was a walk through the woods from our house, and it provided some relief from the heat of August. The hole wasn't very deep, and it would become really murky after we'd splashed around for a while.

Another place — which was much nicer — was an old water dam. This was located off Mountain

Road Number 3, a few miles from where I grew up. You had to park along the road and hike into the spot. It was a large stone dam surrounded by forest. One side had a stand of pine trees, really old growth, and they gave us a nice, soft carpet of pine needles.

I liked to use this place as an icebreaker with a new date. I would ask the girl if she wanted to go swimming in a great little hidden place, away from prying eyes. Not too many people knew about the secret "Water Dam."

Soon after I returned from Vietnam and was discharged from the Navy, I came back to my hometown for some R&R, giving myself time to just chill out and decide what had happened to me over there.

One night, I was out and about, and my instincts guided me to a place called "The Deep End." This was a small neighborhood bar that had become popular with the "head" set in Wilkes-Barre and a hangout for the students from the three colleges located in the city.

On that night, I was introduced to my first wife. She was a student at Wilkes College and a New Yorker. She was a very bright and refreshing person who was quick to laugh at my stumbling attempts at sophistication.

After a few preliminary dates, I asked the

all-important question: "Would you like to go swimming at my secret place, the Water Dam?" She said, "Yes," so we went up there one afternoon. It was relatively late when we got there. I guided her down the narrow path that led to the secret place.

We swam and lay out on the pine needles, just enjoying the evening that was upon us.

Finally, during our last swim, we were both overcome by that feeling caused by the massive amounts of hormones flowing through our young bodies. We decided to perform "The Act" right on the bank opposite our little camp. By this time, it was pretty dark, so I couldn't see what was under us — what we were lying on. It just felt soft — some sort of plant life that grew down to the water's edge.

We satisfied our needs and decided to swim across the pond and retrieve our clothing for the hike out.

That's when things started to fall apart.

In the dark, I was having trouble finding the narrow path that led up the side of the mountain and to my automobile. We ended up staggering through the trees and underbrush. We got whipped by branches and cut on our legs by the briers underfoot. But, either by sheer luck or sheer perseverance, we managed to find our way out.

A few hours later, lounging around in her apartment and relating the story to her roommate, we both started to itch. The itch quickly turned into an all-out scratch-fest, and that, in turn, became sheer madness.

We both had poison ivy all over the most sensitive parts of our anatomy. I had it "down there" — as did she. This infection was so bad that we ended up in the hospital, and that, in itself, was a trying and humiliating experience. The doctors and nurses all had to get in on the treatment. If I'm not mistaken, they even shot some photographs of both of our "down there" parts.

I'm telling you: This was *The Hospital Trip From Hell,* and I became the brunt of all the jokes and snide remarks.

We both recovered and went on to have a relationship that lasted several years, but I never again suggested a trip to the secret "Water Dam." We confined our swimming events to pools on campus or the YMCA around the corner.

The moral — if you could call it that — to this story is simple: Check the location before embarking on a romantic encounter at a "secret" swimming hole.

Abuse in Boca

*B*oca Raton, Florida, is the home of Florida Atlantic University.

I found this upper-division school when my New York girlfriend's parents sent her there to finish a Bachelor's degree. The main emphasis at FAU was the School of Education, and that was the area of study that I wanted to pursue.

Money was tight, so I applied for and received an on-campus work-study job. It paid $4/hour, which, back in 1973, was a decent amount of money. The job found me on loan to the various physical-plant entities such as maintenance, painting, landscaping, and structural. It was a part-time position that I'd just show up for in the morning, and they would assign me to whoever needed labor for that particular day.

The Maintenance Department was broken down into various trades: electrical, plumbing, and structural. I was sent over to plumbing one day and pretty much stayed there for a while.

There was a plumber there, Vinny, and he was from Brooklyn, New York — Vinny, the Brooklyn plumber.

Now, you must understand that Vinny liked me because I called him "Boss" — as in, "OK, Boss" or "What's next, Boss?" — things like that. He figured that I was just another dumb college kid. So, when I was sent over to Maintenance, Vinny would ask for me. I was the gopher. Vinny would send me back and forth to the truck a few dozen times for every job we did. He had this wooden toolbox that I carried around behind him all the time, no matter what we were supposed to be doing.

Vinny was the type of guy who always had one of those dirty little jokes in his wallet, like a really bad photocopy of some guy with an enormous penis. He would stop by the business office and go around showing all the girls his new dirty joke, and I would follow him with the trusty toolbox, just in case someone would question our intentions.

One area that was really big at FAU was the grounds department. The campus was built on an old World War Two runway and had a lot of grassy areas — and what came with grass in South Florida were sprinkler systems. There would be large areas, usually the size of football fields, covered with grass. Every day the sprinklers would come on with their *sput, sput, sput* and spray brackish water all over the place, turning the buildings orange, which the painting department would have to paint white again every six months.

One day Vinny and I got into the truck and made our way over to the Ocean Science Building to fix a dripping faucet. There we were, standing next to this blank wall with a solid metal door and a regular outside spigot that just dripped. Vinny pulled out his big key ring and rummaged through them until he found the right key and opened the door.

Vinny said, "OK, kid — bring the toolbox, and let's take a look at this bastard." We went down into this giant tunnel. As it turned out, the entire campus was connected with these underground tunnels. They carried all of the life-support systems: the chilled water for all the air conditioning, the fresh water, and some really big wires that looked like they could power the entire planet.

While I went out to the truck for a monkey wrench, I noticed that all of the head honchos for the grounds department — along with a crew of workers — were standing in the middle of a field. It was one of those grassy areas that I mentioned earlier. They had just finished installing a new sprinkler system and had sodded the field. I grabbed Vinny's favorite monkey wrench and went back down into the tunnel.

Above our heads were all of these really big pipes. Some were painted blue, others yellow, and a few were red. I knew from my time in the Navy that this color coding was for indicating what ran through each pipe. A few steps from the door were these equally giant valves. Vinny just picked one out and told me to turn it closed.

I asked him, "Are you sure that this is the right valve, Boss?"

He basically told me to shut up. "Looky here, kid: I've been doin' plumbing since your muddah was just thinkin' about youse — *capiche?*"

So, I closed the giant valve.

Vinny decided that it was a done deal and told me to grab the toolbox and go back outside.

We both exited the tunnel at about the same time. There in front of us was a scene straight out of Yellowstone National Park.

The entire area of grass had geysers shooting water about 40 feet into the air, and all of the suits and workers were standing in the middle, getting soaked.

Vinny's cigar flew out of his mouth, and I dropped the toolbox.

When I finally found my voice, I asked, "Hey, Boss: Whadda we do now?"

Vinny said, "Grab the toolbox, and let's get the fuck outta here!"

I think Vinny went back to Brooklyn soon after that.

Construction Humor

*A*s mentioned in various stories throughout this book, I grew up in the trucking and excavating business and learned to operate large machines.

We literally moved mountains and made lakes. For all of the years that I spent pushing dirt around, there was one constant that I noticed: Construction workers have a strange sense of humor, to say the least. Gerald Ford could bash his head on an airplane door, and, within hours, there would be a joke about it circulating around the job site.

In South Florida, I worked for two outfits. One was Hard Drives, and, as the name implies, these guys didn't laugh about very much. Just say it a few times — Hard Drives! When I operated bulldozers for them, I was just a number. I know that for a fact because I was told that I was just a number.

Some of the work was mind-numbing. Have

you ever seen a compacting roller? They go about the job site at 2 miles per hour and beat the ground for compaction. On one job, we were putting in a pad for a new bank building down in Delray Beach, and I had to compact the ground that it would stand on. For a week, I went back and forth at 2 miles per hour, beating the earth — *thump! thump! thump!*

One day, I decided to have lunch at the McDonald's across the street from the site.

While I was standing at the counter, the manager came over and asked me when we were going to be finished. I told him that the guy who determines the compaction ratio would decide that.

He said, "I hope it's going to be soon. When you go back and forth, all of the French fries jump out of their bags."

The other firm I worked for was Shaw Trucking. They were a bit more humane to deal with. At the end of a big project, they would bring a few cases of beer to the site for us workers. With the first company, Hard Drives, we were lucky if they even acknowledged that we were finished.

When I quit Hard Drives, I parked the machine at noon, got into my pickup truck, and drove home. A week later, I went to the office to pick up my last paycheck, and the boss man told me, "We were grooming you for a supervisor's role because you had a college education. And another thing — most guys, when they quit, usually finish out the day."

I replied that he was lucky that I shut the machine off when I left — let alone finish the workday.

At Shaw Trucking, when they were slow with work for the bulldozers, they would put me in a truck. I didn't mind at all being put into a truck — it was a good change of pace and scenery.

One day, I was backing into an area alongside a new beachfront project in Fort Lauderdale. The guys on the building kept waving me back. Unbeknown to me, there was a Job Johnny square in the middle of the dump truck's path, so I could never have seen it. They backed me into it on purpose. When I hit the thing, a Haitian worker came flying out with his pants down around his knees and his little yellow hard hat bouncing on his head.

You see — to these rednecks, that was just "goofing off" — demolishing a Job Johnny with a Haitian worker still inside it.

For me, the real joke was that the Haitian guy could hide in there for 20 minutes or more at a time in the first place. That was just unbelievable. Those places were simply vile. With the Florida heat in that enclosed space and the stench, I still don't know how he did it.

Shaw Trucking had one of those vibrating compacting rollers. These things had a large drum on the front, and it would thump the ground thousands of time per minute. That was how they worked — at a really slow speed, this giant roller would just beat the hell out of the earth.

They sent me out on a job in Boca Raton. It was the new library parking lot. As it turned out, the boss at that job got into a fight with the inspectors — not a very smart thing to do, I can assure you. So, my supervisor told me, "Jason, that guy is in trouble, and we have a lot of money tied up in this job, which we won't see until the parking lot passes muster. So, go down there and whack the crap out of that lot until it's like concrete. Got it?"

Right next to the new parking lot were the city tennis courts. All day long, as I went back and forth, beating the ground, these women were walking around the entrance of the new lot to get to the tennis courts. I started to notice that they had these weird little smiles on their faces. I had nothing better to think about, so I just made a mental note of this and went about my business.

One day, I was talking with this old guy

who worked for Shaw. I told him about my observations, and he laughed.

He said, "You don't get it, do you? Have you ever stood next to that thing when it is running?"

I said, "No," of course. I was always on the machine.

The guy went on to say, "It vibrates the entire ground for 50 yards or more. Don't you understand what these women were experiencing?"

Then it dawned on me, of course. The "French fries" jumping out of the bags.

This giant machine had turned into a huge dildo.

Man — talk about cheap thrills.

The Backhoe on LSD

*I*f I am not mistaken, I related this story in my book a. *PUZZLED EXISTENCE*, but for the benefit of those of you who haven't read that book, I will retell this now.

Louie and I were the premier LSD dealers in the greater Wilkes-Barre area back in 1967/1968. We used to drive down to Hell's Kitchen in New York or out to Boston's South Side to score shoebox-size quantities of acid and sell the stuff around town. We made a lot of money, but, as Jimmy Buffet once sang, *"Made enough money to buy Miami/and pissed it away so fast."*

I was running the backhoe down in Kingston, Pennsylvania, one day. It happened to be a Friday, to be exact, and I had been on this job the whole week. It entailed digging around an entire house to expose the foundation walls. The owner wanted to seal the walls to keep water from coming in. He could have saved himself a lot of money and aggravation if he had listened to us. The house he'd bought was on filled ground near the Susquehanna River. This piece of land would always fill a basement because of the proximity of the river, but he figured that he could accomplish the impossible. So, who were we to argue with that?

Louie and I had gotten in some very potent LSD. It had some fancy name — well, they all had names like "Purple Haze," "Microdot," "Clinical White," and, of course, "Blotter." This stuff was called "Sunshine Barrel." It was shaped like a little orange drum. The one characteristic of this particular mind-fuck was the fact that it took a long time to get you off — up to two hours, in some cases.

It was getting toward quitting time, about 3:30 p.m., if my memory serves me correctly, so I decided to drop the "hit" of acid. My reasoning was simple: I take the acid, work until 4:00, run home, grab a quick shower, and off I would go onto another astral plane. Somewhere between Saturn and Pluto.

I kept digging until 4:00 p.m. and started to shut the machine down for the weekend. Suddenly, the homeowner came out and literally begged me to keep working. There was about 12 feet more to go before the entire foundation would be exposed. It made sense: That way, he would have the entire thing ready for the backfill on Monday. Another determining factor was the $100 bill he slipped into my greasy hand. I reluctantly agreed to complete the excavation for him.

When it started to get onto 5:00 p.m., I poured on the juice and popped a few more revs on the engine to expedite this project before the old LSD started to take effect.

Well, "Haste Makes Waste," as they say, and, in the process of speeding up the backhoeing, I banged the side of the foundation wall with my bucket. Fortunately, it didn't do any damage to the wall. It just made a lot of noise.

About 15 minutes later, I saw an ambulance come screaming up to the front door of the house. The guys ran in and carried someone out on a stretcher, and they roared off toward the nearest hospital. I didn't think much of it, because I couldn't really hear anything over the noise of my machine. I simply kept on digging, finished the job at 5:30 p.m., shut down the 'hoe, and got the hell out of there $100 richer.

The next day, I was at our garage, putzing around with a grease gun, when my brother Bill came over and started to chat, Excavator-Man style, with one foot planted on the iron tracks of a bulldozer. He asked me how I'd made out down in Kingston.

I said, "Affirmative. I completed the job with an hour and a half of OT (overtime)."

Then he said the words I can still hear to this day: "Did you notice anything strange going on?"

I said, "No." I was thinking that maybe he'd heard about the extra C-note that the homeowner had slipped me.

Bill went on to say, "Well, the old lady was sitting by a window, watching you dig, and she had a heart attack right there in her rocking chair."

I immediately cringed. *"Sonofabitch!"* Very carefully, I asked, "Did she make it?"

Bill said, "Yeah. They saved her, but she's still in the hospital."

Then Bill asked me the question I had been dreading during the entire conversation.

"Jason, you didn't, by any chance, whack the side of the house, did you?"

Naturally, I took offense and started shouting four-letter words and asserting how I was a consummate professional and all.

All the while, I was thanking the backhoe gods that it hadn't been a fatal event.

Of Dogs and Sports cars

My brother Mark preferred driving one of his old Porsches. He had a few of them — the old "bathtub" models from the early 1960s. They were in various stages of decay and restoration, depending on the day you were looking at them.

But, for a while, he drove an MGB. These are English cars; they were rugged and handled well, but they had a history of poor electrical systems provided by "Lucas Electric." Just say those words to any MGB owner, and you will see their eyes roll immediately.

Mark put his MGB in our auto-body garage and came up with a paint color that we all dubbed "Burple." It was one of the weirdest shades of purple that anyone had ever seen.

Anyway, that was the car that I borrowed on the fateful day.

Another thing that Mark excelled at was training his big dogs. He would start with them as puppies and go from there. He had quite a few nice dogs. One of them was a long-haired Saint Bernard named "Moses." Mark gave Moses to my parents, and the animal lived on the hill just outside the main kitchen window, where he could sit and watch everything that was going on inside. Moses was a strange dog. He was extremely intelligent and loved to eat bananas. He was a big dog, and his thick, luxuriant coat made him look even larger.

One beautiful Summer afternoon in Wilkes-Barre — a very rare occurrence, I can assure you — I borrowed Mark's "Burple" MGB and decided to take Moses for a ride. Now, you must understand that this dog was so big that the only thing I could do was sit him in the passenger seat of the MGB with the convertible top down. Even then, his head almost stuck up above the windscreen. It was quite a sight: This big, hairy dog, with the look of a philosopher on his face, sitting in this tiny, weird-colored sports car, cruising down the road with his tongue hanging out, slobber blowing back on the cars behind us.

Just across the river from the city of Wilkes-Barre is a large park — Kirby Park. In the summertime, it was the place to be. The place had more than a little history about it. The coal barons had hired the famed landscape architect and writer Frederick Law Olmsted to design the place. He was the same park architect who had designed Central Park in Manhattan, New York City. Coal barons could afford to be generous with money earned on the backs of impoverished coal miners.

But that is another story entirely.

Anyway, I decided to drive Moses down to Kirby Park, which — now that I contemplate it — may not have been one of my better ideas. I drove in, and, of course, there were a lot of young women around who went around the bend when they saw my partner Moses. About three of these sweet little girls started to make a fuss over him, rubbing his head and pulling his ears — a natural reaction to seeing this big, lovable Saint Bernard sitting in a purple sports car.

The only problem was that Moses started to enjoy the attention a little too well. He was literally shaking with excitement, and, on top of that, he got this huge hard-on. Honest to God, his penis was probably bigger than mine. Undoubtedly, that was why I got all upset — it was sheer jealousy. Here was Moses, drooling and shaking, with his huge pink dick flopping around on the leather bucket seat.

The girls just loved it. Needless to say, I never even thought about letting him out of the car.

That would have been more than I could endure at the moment.

Dining Out in New York City

*W*ay back when, I used to be 22 years old. Trust me — it's true. At one time, I was actually a young man with brown, wavy hair. During this period of time, I was living with the woman who would become my first wife. We had an apartment in Wilkes-Barre, but every weekend, we would drive down to New York to visit her father. Her father and mother were divorced. We spent every other weekend in the city, and, on the alternate weekends, we would go out to Long Island and spend the weekend there, visiting her mother.

There I was, a coal-country bumpkin running around New York City without enough sense to look down once in a while. Human sidewalk traffic in New York City is much like highway traffic anywhere else: There is a proper protocol for walking the sidewalks in New York City, with lanes of people going both ways. New Yorkers do not appreciate the occasional person — like me — who walk against the flow of foot traffic. They let you know about it, right on the spot.

"Hey — stoopid! Get over in the right lane! What's a matta' wit you, huh?"

My lady friend's father was a big-shot doctor — a well-known psychiatrist. He had patients who would fly in from, say, Chicago, just for one visit per week. His apartment and office occupied the entire fourth floor of a building on Park Avenue and 72nd St. They had a doorman, an elevator operator, and a maid. I was slow to be impressed — or, at least, I tried to act like I wasn't impressed — while all the while my eyeballs were bulging in their sockets.

Just think — you walk up to the door, and this man opens it for you. I was expecting him to slam me up against the wall and say, "Spread 'em, pal."

But, no. After he learned your name, he would actually say something like, "Good afternoon, Mr. Goodman" or "How is your day going?" I would duly repond by saying something completely asinine. Well — you get the picture: It was a very classy type of residence.

The good doctor liked me because we had both served on a US Navy LST — a boat designed to storm the beaches of Normandy and Okinawa during World War Two. Mine was a rust bucket, but his was brand new — he'd served during World War Two, and I'd served during the Vietnam War.

Our camaraderie would last only as long as it took him to drain his second water-glass full of Jack Daniels. The he would shout at me and threaten to beat my head in with a lead pipe for screwing his daughter. So, I would eat fast, as this usually played out while the maid was serving dinner in his apartment. Then, I would run out and pop over to The Wiffenpoof Bar on Lexington Avenue and drink Watney's Red Barrel Ale until the coast was clear.

But, on rare occasions, he would ask us all out to dinner. One night, we went to a very fancy French restaurant a few blocks from the apartment. For an appetizer, the doctor would order escargot for everyone at the table. This was another first for me. If my dad could have seen me eating snails, I'm sure his commentary would have proven very interesting, to say the least.

After the usual one-hour wait for our appetizers to come out, the garçon placed them on the table, and everyone was given a real pair of pliers. These things looked like the device that women use to curl their eyelashes, though I know now that they were more specialized than that.

I had never had escargot in my life before, and,

to top it off, these were the real deal — they were still clinging to their shells inside. So, rather than ask someone how to use these alien devices, I tried to wing it on my own — acting like the big shot/ "…shaken — not stirred…"/worldly guy I imagined myself to be.

Sure enough, this display of ego and bravado had its consequences. One escargot flew across the room and landed on a table about 15 feet away. I was mortified! *How can something like this happen to Mr. Bond — James Bond?*

So, I asked my host what I should do about this small impropriety, and the doctor said, "You are going to go over there and retrieve that escargot — that's what you're going to do. *Those things are costing me $2.50 apiece!*"

I had to get up and walk over to this table. There was my errant escargot, lying on the table, wedged between the salt-and-pepper shakers, and dripping garlic-infused oil all over their clean, white tablecloth.

"Excuse me — I do believe that's my escargot lying there. If you don't mind…."

I'm sure Bond — James Bond — would have figured out a much more suave way to salve over the embarrassment.

Have I Told You About Me?

*I*n 1968, when I enlisted in the United States Navy, they were all about tradition. For example, while at boot camp in the Great Lakes, we had to wash our own clothes. They had a special room with waist-level sinks where you'd beat your clothes and rubbed them back and forth on a bumpy marble washboard.

But the Navy didn't use ordinary clothespins like the rest of mankind. They employed these small pieces of rope that had little metal bands on each end to keep the threads from fraying. I remember us being restricted if the bows that we tied on the clothesline did not line up perfectly. Our master wanted to be able to stand on the end and sight down the line of bows and see every bow — like the challenge that Odysseus presented to the deadbeats who were living in his house and drinking all of his booze — not to mention what they wanted to do to his wife, Penelope.

Another thing the Navy was very explicit about was our shaving. While we were in boot camp, our faces had to be shaved down to the subcutaneous level, even if it meant bleeding to death. I mean, you would present a very shipshape corpse when they came to carry your body away.

The prescribed shaver of the day was the Gillette "Safety Razor."

Wait. Allow me to repeat that: "Safety Razor."

This thing had a little knob on the bottom of the handle. When you turned it, two little doors would open on top. They looked like the bomb-bay doors on a B-17 if you held it upside down. You would insert a razor blade that was sharpened on both sides. It was referred to as a "Double-Bladed Razor."

This all sounds very civilized until you consider the facts of the matter. First of all, the razor weighed six pounds. I'm exaggerating, of course, but it was very heavy, which affected the way you spun it around your face.

Secondly, handling a "Double-Bladed Razor" was not something you attempted if you had a hangover — or less-than-perfect concentration. If you were foolish enough to take up your blade for even an instant, well, I need not supply too many details of the ramifications of carelessly wielding an extremely sharp, double-bladed instrument of mass destruction. It was not uncommon to walk away from the mirror after shaving with 4 to 6 cuts on your face.

Right after I got home from Vietnam, I was preparing to go out to my favorite cocktail lounge, Visipi's. What made Visipi's so interesting was the fact that it was a gay bar back in the days when there weren't any gay bars. Everyone knew that the gays went to Visipi's and just left them alone. I went there because of the women. A lot of women like to be around gay men because the guys never hit on them, and they could feel comfortable.

Except for me. I went there to hit on women who, after a few drinks, were reconsidering their decision to hang out in a gay bar in the first place. Voila! Here I was, right in their faces — a heterosexual man just teeming with testosterone.

Well, I was at my parents' house, preparing for a night of earthly delights at Visipi's. I went into the bathroom to shower and shave. In 1970, the three-day-old-stubble look just didn't cut it with the opposite sex the way it seems to today. Women would just take one look and think, *Loser.*

The only problem was the fact that I had only my official US Navy shaving kit — with the infamous "Gillette Safety Razor." So, I managed to drop in a brand-new Double-Bladed Razor Blade without the need for a tourniquet and proceeded to shave my face. Naturally, I left the mirror with 6 cuts on my face. Fortunately, I was able to stop the bleeding with the use of a stiptic pen and little balls of toilet tissue.

I was all dressed up, standing at the bar at Visipi's, chatting up a few girls. Leo, my favorite bartender, fixed me up with a nice cold cocktail. Everything was as it should be — except for the reaction of the girls. They were sort of fascinated by my face and kept staring at me intensely.

After about an hour, the tonic portion of my beverage asked to be relieved, and I headed to the men's room. As it was a men's room in a gay bar, it was covered with mirrors from floor to ceiling. There, I encountered my image: A studly 20-ish-year-old male, well dressed in a black turtleneck sweater and nice slacks.

My face was another matter. I'd forgotten to remove the little balls of toilet tissue. They glared out at me in the mirror like so many flareups of serious acne.

This, I concluded to my chagrin, would explain why those women had been staring at me with such intensity.

Bill Mows the Lawn

My brother Bill had a few weird quirks.

He did not like dogs or the smell of fruit. In the 60 years that I knew him, I don't think I ever saw him actually eat even one piece of fruit.

He also disliked trees. That isn't as strange as it sounds — he just didn't like trees. The painter and Art Nouveau icon Mondrian hated trees, too. In fact, anything green really disturbed Mondrian. It is said that he bought a lot next to his studio just so he could cut down a tree that blocked one of his window views.

But my brother Bill did have his own strange behaviors.

He bought a house — an old double-block situated on a corner lot in the town of Edwardsville. We demolished the house and cleared the lot. Then Bill had a small, two-bedroom home constructed on the lot. The one thing that he never got around to doing was the yard. He never landscaped — or even planted grass — for the more than 25 years that he lived in the house. In our father's business, we used to install huge yards, plant grass, add a few well-placed boulders for effect and basically cover the earth with another man's burden.

One day, while servicing the machines at our garage, Bill came in and asked me to take the small bulldozer down to his house in Edwardsville. I had enough sense back then not to ask why, but, eventually, he told me that he'd received a certified letter from the borough.

So, I loaded the machine onto the trailer and dropped it off at Bill's house. A few minutes later, he rolled in and jumped onto the machine and proceeded to scrape up all of the weeds into a large pile in the back. Then we brought in one of our backhoes, loaded the pile onto a truck, and hauled it away.

When everything was said and done, Bill stood there looking at his bare dirt yard and exclaimed, "There. I just mowed my yard for another year!"

Every year, the borough would send him threatening letters. At first, they would just come through the regular mail. Then, after a few more weeks, the certified letters would begin, until Bill decided to "mow the lawn."

He had studied Transcendental Meditation for a few years and came to the conclusion that weeds were another of man's flowers.

At any rate, I'm sure the borough preferred looking at raw dirt rather than a nice, manicured lawn.

Anatomy in a Hotel Lobby

The man from whom I rent a house in Westport, Ireland, was gracious enough to allow me to use his car. It was a Volkswagen Passat, which, in Ireland, is a high-level automobile, a very classy ride, you might say.

For the more than 26 years that we have been living in Ireland, we have never gone to Northern Ireland. Years ago, I made a wrong turn and came upon a road that was blocked by one of those red-and-white-striped poles that action-movie stars love to drive cars through at great speed. On both sides of this roadblock stood two soldiers. Both were carrying submachine guns, and both were dressed in full battle gear. My impression was that, at a certain time in my life, I was paid extra to be in a war zone in Vietnam, and I wasn't going to spend time or money in a place where they have armed guards at the border.

But, in 2015, they had softened the border

between the Republic of Ireland and Northern Ireland, so the armed guards were gone. My personal feelings are that the British should just give these counties back to Ireland and pull out of that island. But, in reality, that's going to happen only when snowballs no longer melt in Hell.

And, speaking of balls, here's what happened that day.

We were in a town called Letterkenny, which is way up North, only 15 klicks from the border. Our plan was that, on the following morning, we would be traveling through Northern Ireland on a trip to see the Giant's Causeway outside of Derry.

Teresa and I were standing in the hotel lobby, finalizing our two-night stay. It was a place that we'd stayed at before on another trip up North, and we were familiar with the hotel. About 15 feet away were the two stainless steel elevators. I was going about the business of trying to remember the license plate number of the car we were using when the elevator doors opened with the *Ding!* of a bell.

We glanced over in that direction, and out of the elevator stepped a large penis. This thing was at least 7 feet tall and came complete with two hairy gonads at its base. The big penis then proceeded to walk through the lobby and into the bar and lounge. Everyone around us, ourselves included, were somewhat aghast. It's not every day that a 7-foot penis steps out of a hotel elevator.

As it turned out, there was a person inside this giant penis. It was a costume of sorts being worn as part of a wedding that was taking place elsewhere in the hotel. We got our room key and went upstairs to park our suitcases. When we returned to the lobby, the penis was somewhat deflated and sitting in a heap behind the front desk. From what I could gather, the manager of the hotel had gone completely ballistic at the thought of a huge dick walking around his hotel and had confiscated the penis — foreskin, gonads, and all. He had placed the errant member in custody until after the wedding had been consummated — or, let's just say until the contract had been signed.

One Night in Ireland

*T*here is an expression used in Ireland that parallels a few of our own. When we say, "What's happening?" or "How's it going?" the Irish would say, "How are ye gettin' on?"

My wife and I heard this expression many times over the course of our many trips to Ireland. But we never heard it in quite the same way as we did one night in Westport.

The town of Westport, Ireland, has an octagon, a place where three major roads meet and which anchors the shopping district of the town. There are four pubs, a hotel, some shops, and your standard granite penis with some guy standing on top. It is held up by a massive pedestal surrounded by park benches and seagulls.

Besides the semi-circular parking area, there are a few old buildings. Of course, when you say the word "old" in Ireland, it doesn't mean the same thing as when the word is used here in the United States. In the U.S., something "old" means that it dates back maybe 250 years. In Ireland, "old" usually denotes a building that is at least 500 years old. My house in Lititz, Pennsylvania, was built in 1908. Once, in the course of a conversation, I referred to it as being "old," and my Irish friends just laughed and told me, "Aye — shut yer gob. That's a mere baby by our standards." To them, a 100-plus-year-old house is a modern subdivision, and their "sticky stone" around the entrance is very real.

One of the buildings on the octagon was the old town hall. It dated back about five centuries and was in a bad way. Over the course of four years, the people of Westport pretty much gutted the entire building and rebuilt it, from the basement up to the roof.

Anyway, they finished the project on the town hall in 2016. One interesting thing they did was to build a very nice, modern theatre into the structure. It is fully equipped with a good sound system, steep, angled seating, posh seats, and a nice stage. In adding the theatre, the town fathers built a source of income into this new community building. All year, they offer various musical programs and other productions. It's really a nice little theatre. It probably seats 500, maybe more.

One night we had tickets for a traditional-music presentation at the newly renovated town hall. Prior to the show, I had taken my wife downtown for a nice meal at one of our local haunts — the old "dinner and a show" routine, which she enjoys. It's another night away from the pots and pans in our kitchen. We left the restaurant at about 7:45 pm, walking up Bridge Street toward the theatre and had just passed Matt Malloy's Pub. Matt Malloy plays flute with "The Chieftains," a well-known Irish music group who toured the world and produced a number of albums. Malloy's association with The Chieftains made his pub quite popular.

Just above Matt Malloy's Pub, a young guy cut across the street and walked right up to us. He stopped and said, "What did the horse say to the one-legged jockey?"

We both looked at him blankly. Neither of us had any idea what the punchline might be.

The guy said, "How are ye gettin' on?"

Then he turned and continued walking down Bridge Street in the direction of Matt Malloy's Pub. No introduction, no fuss, no "Goodbye." The guy had just walked up, told us his joke, and then just continued on his way.

We both stood there on the sidewalk, trying to decipher exactly what had just happened. I had no idea who the guy was. I'd never seen him before in my life. He'd stopped us in the middle of the sidewalk on Bridge Street, Westport, Ireland, just to tell us a joke.

It was beautiful, we both commented. This was the type of encounter that is among the reasons that help define why we live in Ireland every year.

A Murder of Babushkas

*T*here are a number of stories in this book that pertain to the heavy-equipment industry. Considering that I grew up working in that business all across the United States and sustained myself doing work in that field, it's only natural that I would draw on that experience for material for this book. This line of work has been the source of many an interesting event over the years. Here is one of them.

We had contracts with various boroughs and municipalities around our area. One of them was the town of Edwardsville. No one has ever claimed that borough employees are all Rhodes Scholars. Far from it. Some of these guys excelled at creating the most perfect beer bellies I have ever seen. You can achieve that form of belly only with years of rigorous training — hours of standing around leaning on a shovel and copious amounts of beer after a hard day on the streets keeping a dump like Edwardsville safe.

Well, this particular day had started out fairly well. I showed up. My dad told me to take the backhoe and run down to Edwardsville and dig up the street for them. Apparently, they were having a problem with the sewer line on Church Street. (Why they called it "Church Street" will always be a mystery to me — there is not one church on that street.)

So, I drove the machine down there. A jackhammer crew had already busted up the asphalt. I dug a hole about 15 feet deep to locate the sewer line. It never failed to amaze me that you could have six guys with those beautiful beer bellies standing around staring at a hole in the ground — while there was only one man down in the bottom of the hole actually doing any work.

It was an old terra cotta line — a big one, too. This is what is called a "main." They proceeded to bust a hole in the side of the clay pipe and look up into the darkness — or, should I say, "dungness."

They all boarded their two borough vehicles and decided to run down the street to Kowalski's tavern for a little liquid lunch.

I sat on my machine eating a football meat sandwich and drinking lukewarm thermos coffee. You probably want to know what "football meat" is. Well, it's plain, old, cheap-as-dirt Bologna.

After an hour, my boozy coworkers returned from their executive lunch and went back to staring down at the terra cotta sewer pipe. One of the guys, a self-styled foreman of sorts, decided to run down to the maintenance garage and get some fire hose. They were going to "flush out" this bastard real good.

You must understand that we were sitting at the bottom of a hill. Right above us, on both sides of the street, as far as the eye could see, were double-block houses. They were stacked up that hill with Germanic precision.

Stanley came back with 100 feet of four-inch fire hose and told Yosh to "hook da bastard up to da hydrant over there. We'll flush dis bastard out real good."

I shouted to Stanley to come over to the machine, and I said to him, "Hey, Stanley — are you sure that this is what you want to do here? Stick that hose up the pipe and all?"

And he said, "Listen, Goodman. We're gonna flush dat bastard out — you got it? Just sit there, and we can backfill this here hole real quick."

I said, "You know what, Stash? Maybe youse should get a camera in there to peek up da pipe a little and take a look-see."

He replied, "Listen, Goodman. Youse run da

backhoe, and I'll flush da bastard out."

"OK, Stash, OK. I was just thinkin' out loud, so to speak."

They pushed that hose up the pipe for about 25 feet. They had a rope tied onto the brass handle of the shutoff valve on the end so that, after they'd gotten the hose up there, they could just pull the rope and let it fly — all 300 psi of pressure from the street fire hydrant.

I could hear the water gushing out. It began as a muffled roar, and it kept getting louder and louder.

After about 15 minutes, I started to see all these women. They were wearing babushkas, and some were carrying rolling pins. They kept coming out of the houses, going all the way up to the hill. There were about a dozen of them, and they didn't appear at all pleased with the events.

I shouted over the roar to Stash, "Hey, Stash! Youse got some company coming down the hill!"

Stanley nearly jumped when he looked up the hill. He told one of his guys to shut the water off and jump in the trucks. They all took off before the ladies reached our location. I was the only person left on the job, just sitting on my backhoe.

As it turned out, all of the toilets and sinks in their houses were spewing water. They said it was like having a fountain or two in your bathroom — and it wasn't the most pleasant water, either. One woman had actually been sitting on the throne when the deluge erupted.

Man, talk about a bidet.

These ladies were going to tear me to shreds until I told them that I was only the machine operator. I told them to call the borough if they wanted to complain.

I'm not a gambling man, but I wonder:

Can you have a full house and a flush in the same hand?

Soiling One's Trousers

*E*xcavating is in itself a very dangerous occupation.

Consider the fact that you are working with these huge machines that can wreck houses, move entire mountains, and leave holes in their place. Over the years, I've had a few close calls while engaged in the art of excavating. This is the story of one of them.

It was a really fine Pennsylvania day — nice temperatures and blue sky all around. My father came up to me and said, "Jason, load up the HD-16 and take it up the mountain to Jesse's quarry. We are going to start hogging out shale on Monday."

The HD-16 was one of the biggest machines we had. It was a giant bulldozer, with a set of scaffires on the back. These were huge teeth that dropped down under hydraulic pressure and ripped open the earth. They were used specifically for tearing up rock — in this case, shale, the stuff used for road bases.

I fired up the 'dozer and very carefully loaded it onto our equally large truck and trailer. Then I chained the thing down so it wouldn't just slide off when I went around a corner.

We had this big truck called an "N-Series Ford Tractor." It was used for hauling around large pieces of equipment like the HD-16. It had a Detroit Diesel engine and two transmissions. One was the regular 5-speed, and the other had 4 different gears in it: High, High-Low, Low, and Low-Low.

Larksville Mountain was a real mountain. At some points, the road seemed to go straight up into the sky, and it had a bunch of twists and turns. I started out at the bottom and shifted the transmissions into First Gear and Low, respectively. Then I started up the road. The engine was screaming as only a Detroit Diesel can.

Everything was going well. I looked in my rearview mirrors and saw just a big, iron blade in both of them. I roared up the mountain and passed the first graveyard, where the real hump started. As I got about halfway up the "hump," the engine started to bog down. I was losing power quickly.

Now, the truck had a Maxi-Brake that locked up the trailer with air pressure, but I knew that it wouldn't hold on this steep grade and under the weight of this machine.

My problem was simple. I should have put the second transmission in Low-Low gear instead of just Low. So, I reached over, said a short prayer, and slapped the gearshift around into Low-Low. I made it — I actually made the shift. This would have warranted bragging rights under normal circumstances, but I couldn't tell a soul about it now, because it was my fault that it was in Low to begin with!

Suddenly, the entire front of the truck lifted up off the road. I was looking straight up at that pretty blue sky. The thought went through my head: If this bulldozer cuts loose, it could kill someone. Nothing would have stopped its backward momentum as it rolled, out of control, down the mountain and through the houses below.

There was nothing that I could do but sit there with the engine roaring away.

Then it happened.

The front of the truck ever so slowly just went back down onto the road.

I reached the knob of the hill just as I came up the road. On a flat spot, I stopped the truck to get my thoughts together and drank some thermos coffee. As I stepped off the truck, I noticed that my trousers were a little damp in the area of my urine maker.

The Big Duke and Fast Thinking

*T*he HD-16 made it to Jesse's quarry in one piece. I hauled that monster up Larksville Mountain and arrived with slightly wet bluejeans and a racing heart.

We were engaged in the process of building 3.8 miles of road for the borough of Jackson Township. It was called "Jesse's Road" and went from RD#2 Mountain Road over to and connecting to RD#3 Road. First, my brother Bill ripped up a big pile of shale. He spent the entire week doing this before we came in with trucks and bulldozers to lay it down.

We first chain-sawed all the trees in our path; then we pushed out all the stumps. Then we scooped up whatever topsoil there was and hauled that away to be resold. This was to be a two-lane country road that went up hills and wiggled through the woods until it met up with RD#3.

When you build a road from scratch, you have

to lay in a really good base. That's what the shale was for — the road base material. We hauled it in and spread it out about two feet thick. Then the final-grade bulldozer would flatten it out and a roller would compact the surface. Later on, they would come in and pave it.

As we were working, we came to the base of a hill with a curve at its base. My brother Mark was operating the bulldozer, and he kept signaling to dump more and more shale in one particular place. I finally got out of the truck and asked him what the hell he was doing, using up all of this material on this one curve.

Mark told me, "Listen, Dog Breath. They are eventually going to pave this thing — correct? Well, I want to come screaming down that hill in my Porsche and make this curve without piling into the trees. So, just keep bringing in the shale until I tell you to stop."

What he was doing was "banking" the curve. You just can't put down a flat road on a corner or curve unless the speed limit is 5 mph. If it isn't banked correctly, you'll go flying off the road. That is what he was doing — piling up the shale on one side of the curve and placing an extreme angle on it.

Which was all well and good until my father — "The Big Duke" — showed up.

Naturally, he sought me out because Mark was his favorite. With The Duke, whatever was wrong had to be my fault, no matter what.

Well, The Duke started shouting and cursing, calling me every name in the book that meant "stupid" — and then some. He was yelling, "What in the hell are you doing here with all of this shale? You should be at least a quarter mile further along with this road by now!"

Then he went into another tirade about how dumb I was, until he ran out of breath and I had the opportunity to say, "But, Dad. If it's wrong, well, it was you who taught me everything I know. Do you remember telling me that my whole life?"

He stopped, looked around, and just turned and jumped in his pickup truck and sped off down the new road.

Welfare Wives

*A*llow me to tell a story in memory of my good friend Charles Feldman.

Charles owned a huge Volkswagen dealership in Kingston, Pennsylvania. That is where he made his money. He was also a man of letters and an art collector. In fact, that's how we met. I sold him some of my paintings — actually, I traded them for automobiles.

Charles fell in with some really dubious characters. If you want the truth, they were scumbags. Charles was talked into investing, silently, in a construction company that had just landed almost $4 million worth of HUD contracts. These entailed four major jobs, two firehouses, 16 low-income housing renovations and a spruce-up of another low-income housing complex, repairing and replacing sidewalks, retaining walls, etc.

That job, the housing complex, was located in Lower Askum, an area south of Wilkes-Barre.

There, they were supposed to replace all of the concrete sidewalks. The only problem was this: Stinky, the General Manager that I replaced, had a bad habit of snorting cocaine and then going on the job site and saying rather nasty things about the HUD inspector — you know: commentary about the size of the man's penis, or what he had done to the guy's mother and wife the night before. Things like that.

Any sensible person would have ventured to ask "Why?" Stinky was not a very nice person. He cost Charles more than a quarter-million dollars and then died violently when he and his cohort pulled out in front of a speeding tractor-trailer one day.

Before Stinky's early demise, Charles asked me to replace Stinky in his capacity as General Manager of the building firm, which I did — very reluctantly, I might add. All of the projects were in various stages of completion, and all of the inspectors tended to ignore many of my phone calls.

I put a crew down in Lower Askum to jackhammer out the sidewalks that my predecessor had recently installed. As I walked the job site with my very combative HUD inspector, he implied that, for $500, my problems could all go away.

I went to Charles and told him I needed $500. He asked, "For what?" and I told him. To his credit, he threw me out of his office and told me never — I repeat, never — again ask him to pay a bribe. In Wilkes-Barre, if you wanted to accomplish anything, you had to pay bribes. The place is so despicably corrupt — it's just how they do business there. Charles was aware of this and refused to be a part of it.

I hired my brothers to do the excavating. "To the victors go the spoils," as they said in ancient Rome. Mark was operating the machine. He was working in an area close to one of those freestanding mailboxes — the ones with all the little cubbyholes that you need a key to access. He reached out and under the mailboxes with the bucket of the machine to remove some chunks of concrete. The bucket bumped the bottom of this mailbox extraordinaire, and it locked up. It had a failsafe mechanism on it that shut the thing down if it was tampered with.

Now, that, in itself, would not have been an issue, except the day on which this occurred just happened to be welfare-check-delivery day. At about 3:00 p.m., all of these unemployed CEOs and consultants would come out en masse to receive their stipends. They discovered that their keys would not open their mailboxes.

Well, they went totally ape on us. I haven't heard screaming like that since the great San Francisco earthquake.

Let me just say that I called the Post Office, and then we left in haste, before this gaggle of hyenas could rip us to shreds.

Prickly Circumstances

There is nothing better suited for that "romantic" date than a picnic under the stars.

But, not just any sky with stars in it — this event was being staged in Boulder, Colorado.

One night, while I was drinking cocktails at Potter's Bar on Broad Street in Boulder, I met two women. One would prove to be my companion for several days, and the other ended up being my second wife.

The blonde was up from Texas on a vacation to visit her friend from times past, the brunette. I used my standard pick-up line on that particular evening, and it worked like a charm: "Hello, girls. Have I told you about me?"

We gathered around Potter's plank and drank a number of exotic cocktails until the closing gong rang out. Blondie decided that she would prefer to go home with me that evening as opposed to her long-lost girlfriend.

I can't say I even fully understood those social

dynamics projected between old girlfriends —
though, at the time, I wasn't complaining, either.

So, she went home with me, and we proceeded
to test the warranty on my black satin sheets
— for the entire evening, I might add. The old
adage states that "Blondes have more fun," and
this young lady was no exception. We proceeded
to enjoy each other's company for that entire
week, right up until her departure from Denver
International Airport.

Ah, the joys of youth!

Needless to say, a few weeks later, I was
diagnosed with a severe case of a very common
sexually transmitted disease. This damaged not
only my checkbook balance but also my sense of
well-being. *"Protection!"* you might say. Well, yes,
but this was the age of the daily birth-control
pill, which rendered self-preservation a moot
subject.

Several weeks later, the brunette darkened
my door, carrying a loaf of homemade bread.
Obviously, my newfound blond petri dish had
provided her with my address prior to winging
back to Texas.

Brunette stayed for a while. We chatted and
listened to music, with a few very strategically
placed glasses of *Moet Extra Brut* — and a
stunning afternoon it turned out to be.

Years later, during our divorce proceedings, I learned that she had left her little purse in my apartment on purpose. This turned out to be the only excuse she needed to return and enter my life completely for the next six years, though all of that nasty business came much later. This story deals with one of our more intimate dates.

In preparation, I went out and bought one of those long-neck bottles of Spanish red wine. This was designed to impress her — that long, slender green bottle poking out of my hiking bag. I also bought a chunk of nice Emmental cheese and a French baguette — the perfect combination for a little romantic supper in the outdoors.

We piled into my English sports car and made our way up into the Rocky Mountains to a very nice, private spot that I was familiar with.

It was a beautiful night, with white fluffy clouds racing across the face of a full moon. My perch was complete with a panoramic view of the Denver city lights off in the distance.

I had a classic woolen blanket. It was cream colored and had "U.S. Navy" emblazoned on it in deep blue. Don't ask me where it came from. Let's just say that I liberated it from a boring existence in some Navy sickbay.

As I threw the blanket open with a great flourish of bravado, a large cloud passed across the moon, and the normally bright lighting was reduced to near darkness. But that throw was successful, and we sat on the U.S. Navy blanket for some bohemian refreshment.

Just as the bra strap came undone and my belt was unfastened, we both noticed a slight prickling sensation on our bottoms and back. This quickly morphed into an all-out assault of sharp stabs into our flesh, some of which left little red dots on my beige woolen blanket.

When the cloud had passed and the moonlight returned, I pulled up our ground cover to find a huge patch of small and rather lethal cactus right under where we had been lying.

My well-calculated "Bohemian" picnic had ended on the tip of a cacti rapier.

Allen Ginsberg's "Howl" was given new meaning that night in Boulder, Colorado.

Kangaroo Court

I interviewed for a position with the Department of Education, Victoria Schools, Melbourne, Australia, in 1976.

This feat required travel from Boca Raton, Florida, where I was enrolled in graduate work, to Madison, Wisconsin, in the dead of winter. The fact that I exposed myself to below-zero conditions, which included snow and ice, to seek a job in Australia, was not lost on the headhunter I met with.

After a few months, they flew me, along with 400 other American secondary-school teachers, to Melbourne for our assignments.

One stupid thing I remember was anti-American demonstrators at the Melbourne International Airport sporting placards telling us to "Go Home!"

Just consider this: In one giant fell swoop, the Education Department populated most of their state-run high schools with state-of-the-art, cutting-edge teachers from the United States. These individuals, including myself, had the benefit of the best training in the world at that time, and it didn't cost them or the taxpayers one thin Australian pence for all of that education.

With that said, I settled in with an apartment and a used automobile, and then proceeded to pretend that I actually knew what I was doing.

One evening, while driving home from the pub, I was involved in a simple little fender-bender with another individual who just happened to pull out in front of me and stop. As time went on, I came to realize that Australian drivers left a little to be desired in the realm of experience and common sense.

Well, that little mishap attracted the attention of the local constabulary, and they decided that I was the one who would be ticketed for this debacle.

Naturally, I was offended by their decision and decided to fight this thing in court. With hindsight securely in place, I can honestly say that it wasn't one of my better judgment calls, but I went ahead with my visit to the supreme court of Australia.

Well, I soon discovered that you could not just stroll into a courtroom and demand justice. In Australia, you have to hire both a "barrister" and a "solicitor." One peson did all of the paperwork — discovery, witness tampering, bribe-paying, etc., while the other went into the courtroom and argued your case.

Three thousand dollars later, I had my day in court. (And that was in 1976 Australian currency.)

My solicitor told me to meet him early at the courthouse because he wasn't certain what number we would be on the docket. As most ill-conceived ventures into the status of folly go, my big case was the absolute last one to be heard. This, of course, allowed my judge to sit there all day and listen to fools like me distort the nature of justice. In my own, naïve, uninformed-American way, I thought, *My honorable jurist is undoubtedly well rested after this marathon of legal gymnastics and eager to hear about my thirst for justice. He will most asssuredly take a keen interest in my welfare because of my American status.*

I'm not a judge by any stretch of the imagination, but, after listening to these individuals' cases being presented for a few hours, a person could actually hear the bullshit and the outright lies issuing from the defendants. This experience gave me a greater understanding of what not to say to a judge, especially if you happen to be guilty.

Eventually, my legal education started to wear

thin, and, when they recessed for lunch, I was pleasantly surprised to find a nice pub directly across the street from the courthouse. I decided to have a nice pub lunch, washed down with a few pints of cold bitters. This proved to be my second lapse in judgment that day. The first, of course, was just showing up for this matter of principle.

After a light lunch and an undetermined number of pints, I returned to my seat in the courtroom.

Allow me to explain that, in Australia, they base their legal system on the British model. I mean, the country is part of the British Commonwealth, and they do have pictures of the queen hanging everywhere there is a convenient nail in the wall.

What really fascinated me was the wigs.

That's right — wigs.

Both the judge and the solicitors were all sporting these little white powdered wigs on their heads.

My ingestion of strong Australian beer probably did not help matters, but I found all of this rather amusing. I started out innocently enough, with a few "Phews!" That's the sound that happens when you're holding your breath, but it still sort of escapes and makes that *"Phiff!"* sound.

This progressed into guffaws, and I ended up

holding my sides and my nose at the same time. I just couldn't stop myself. It was just a little too much — these old, pink men, talking away, very seriously, with these little wigs on their heads.

Unfortunately, the judge did not share my enthusiasm, How could he? He was wearing one of those wigs!

Needless to say, I lost my case and ended up paying a fine for contempt of court.

It just didn't seem fair. I was just sitting there, minding my own business.

Hell, they were the ones walking around with powdered wigs on — not me!

The Home Business

*W*hen you're poor, your mind is usually preoccupied with two things: Hunger and money. Allow me to examine these two commodities.

Hunger

We had chickens — quite a few of them. But the problem was that they were "laying" hens, which meant that you couldn't just eat them, or your source of income would disappear. After a while, you become obsessed over getting those food items that you can't have, like real meat and a jar of peanut butter. When I say "real meat," I mean store-bought steaks and ground beef. We usually had some meat products, but they invariably came from the forest: Rabbit, pheasant, and deer meat. The authorities refer to these as "bush meat."

During the summer months, the house was always red — but not due to the kitchen coal stove being stoked. It was canning season. My mother always had some form of food material cooking on top of the stove, along with a large pot that contained the mason jars, being boiled for sanitation reasons. Every year, you would hear about an entire family perishing from some form of botulism caused by bad canning practices.

There would be vegetables, rabbit stew and chunks of venison being prepared for canning. This was our winter larder, and everyone would take a keen interest in what was going on, counting the number of mason jars that ended up on the shelf in the cellar.

Later on in life, during the '60s, I had opportunities to live in hippie communes. I used to tell these people how difficult it was to survive when you were a hunter/gatherer. They would laugh at me with that pot-smoke insincerity and dismiss my comments out of hand — until the winter arrived and they were desperate, trying to gather frozen firewood and make it burn. This lifestyle is not easy. In fact, you will find yourself working from sunup to sundown most days just to stay warm and keep the hunger pangs at bay.

Money

"Poor" literally means "no money." Go ahead — look it up. To be poor: 1) Lacking resources, aka money; 2) Having a wallet; 3) Not having any money to put in that wallet; and 4) Beating up your wife because, somehow, it is her fault that you don't have any money.

Most violent arguments between poor couples start over the question of whether Chopin or Mozart wrote "The Vandenberg Concerto."

Actually, that isn't true.

Most arguments center around not having any money. I know this for a fact because I witnessed this almost every night. A row could start from the innocent statement "I'm hungry." Usually, if you do not have enough money for food, you most definitely don't have enough to go out and get plastered, so that wasn't a viable means of escape.

If you look through the pantry of a poor person, you may find a bag of flour, some rice, and maybe a few shriveled-up potatoes. There won't be much of anything else. Even things like salt and sugar are purchased commodities. Also, the question of credit at your friendly neighborhood grocery store is a moot subject. Very few merchants will extend credit to poor people for the simple reason that they might not get paid.

It is a cycle that keeps repeating itself.

Some would say, "Just go out and get a job." But if you are poor, that is much easier said than done. Poor people don't have the clean clothes, the gasoline for a car — assuming they have a car — or the fare for the bus, all of which are necessary for finding and keeping a job. It isn't as simple as the old expression "God helps those who help themselves." When you are poor, it is almost impossible to help oneself.

For this reason, I became obsessed with owning a successful home business when I was a kid. This was going to be my ticket to riches and a full belly. I realized at an early age that very talented people came from dirty coal towns like Wilkes-Barre, so I figured, Why not me? Why can't I become a huge success? You will note while reading the following paragraphs that there were monumental barriers that had to be overcome on this road to wealth.

Allow me to describe some of my travails.

Candy Making

After glancing through my mother's only cookbook, I found a recipe for homemade caramel. This was it! I would corner the caramel market here in Larksville and become the gooey baron of the caramel trade!

First, allow me to explain how a coal stove works. You start a fire in the firebox using some newspaper — if you have any — and some wood called "kindling." Once the fire gets going, you begin to build up a layer of hot coals in the bottom. This is important because coal does not ignite easily. It needs a lot of help from wood coals first.

After the fire is roaring, you put few small shovels of coal in and keep building it up until you have a nice, hot fire. But it is important to set the "draughts." These are little doors that control the amount of air that passes through your fire. To make the fire burn, you open the bottom and close the top; this forces air to pass. To dampen the fire, you reverse that pattern. This allows just the gas on top of the fire to burn, which, in turn, conserves the fuel in the firebox. Sometimes you can dampen a fire all night, shake down the ash in the morning, add fresh coal, and, Voila! You have a cooking fire without the use of paper and kindling.

When I started my caramel business, I used one of my mother's really good stainless-steel cook pots. It was the type with the copper on the bottom, probably a family heirloom of sorts.

Things were moving along quite well until the fire started to die. Then I was in trouble. The recipe was quite specific about maintaining even heat throughout the process, and I was rapidly losing my heat.

So, I went outside with my pot of caramel and

fired up my dad's acetylene torch. I was standing in the driveway with the pot in one hand and the torch in the other when my dad drove up in his truck.

My father never used the "F" word when we were young, but he made up for this with the side of his size-11 leather boots or his massive open hand. He was definitely not pleased. Even though I knew about his sweet tooth and swore that this effort was on his behalf, he kicked my ass. Then, when my mother came out and saw that I had blackened her cook pot, she proceeded to kick my ass.

Let me just say this: The Hershey Company had nothing to fear after this episode. I was not going to lower their Dow-Jones expectations anytime soon.

The Wreck'em Ade Stand

I came up with another brilliant idea: I was going to make a killing, with a refreshment stand for the weary travelers — all four of them — who trekked up our dusty mountain road.

I needed a flashy location for my refreshment stand and a nice wooden structure to give the feeling of permanence. Around the yard was a pile of old wooden boards. I went to work nailing these together with the determination and confidence of any self-assured tycoon. My stand would morph into the finest restaurant on Larksville Mountain. I would have a *monopoly!*

Just as I was installing one of the final boards — yep, you guessed it — my dad drove up in his truck.

The unfortunate thing was this: He had a small barrel filled with old, bent, rusty nails. Next to it, there was a box of nice, new shiny nails, so I used those because it was a matter of appearances: My stand had to be presentable, and that was not going to happen if I used those old, rusted nails.

After my father kicked my ass, he started jumping up and down on top of my refreshment stand, smashing it to bits. All the while he was doing this, he was shouting, "Here is your refreshment stand! *Just look — I made it portable! Now you can carry it anywhere!"*

My brother Bill was the one who coined the term "Wreck'em Ade," and it stuck. For months afterward, my brothers would ask when my Wreck'em Ade stand was going to open and then burst out laughing, needless to say, at my expense.

Household Cleaners

After seeing the price of a jug of dish soap, I decided to make a fortune in the cleaning-supply business. I would manufacture and sell cleaning products from the basement of our home until the new factory was built. I started by melting bars of Ivory soap and then mixing together different chemicals like ammonia and Clorox.

It was at some point during the process that I realized that a college degree in chemistry would have helped. If I had to guess, I'd say that that point occurred just as I started to pass out from the fumes.

My mother found me and pulled my limp body from the basement. She had to open all of the windows in the house to vent out the toxic Jupiterian atmosphere that I had created by mixing the wrong compounds.

When my parents realized that I was going to live and not have permanent lung or brain damage, they both kicked my ass, and that ended my dream of becoming the next Johnson & Johnson.

I could just see it: *Jason & Jason, Household Cleaning Maggot.*

After these few failed attempts at international trade, I decided to step down from the CEO chair and give a younger executive a chance. I must say: I still had some tremendous ideas — a weekly newspaper, a car-license-plate business, and a few others that I am not at liberty to discuss due to the out-of-court decision.

I gave up venture capital and decided to work for a living. It was a difficult decision but one that had to be made.

It never fails to amaze me that the human ass has the ability to grow back after it has been kicked a number of times.

Maybe that could be my next multinational company! *The Artificial Ass Works.*

A Few *ACTUAL* Ghost Stories

The Marine House

*D*uring the Winter months in Boulder, Colorado, I returned to my home state of Pennsylvania because there was little work. This was the generally accepted procedure in the excavating business. You worked like hell for eight to nine months; then you signed up for unemployment compensation for the entire Winter season. Then you returned in the Spring to work some more.

The most important way this affected me was that I had to give up my apartment on The Hill, so when I returned to Colorado, I had to find a new place to live. As Boulder was such a large University town, my old apartment would reopen during the early part of summer. I needed something temporary.

While driving through downtown, I noticed a sign advertising rooms for rent in a "gentlemen's house." The place was called "The Marine House." Why that was, I haven't a clue. "Marine" usually implies the water, oceans, wooden ships, and iron men — that sort of thing. But this was it — "The Marine House," in the middle of landlocked Boulder.

I rented a series of rooms — two, to be exact — well-lighted spaces with an ample closet. We shared a kitchen and large bathroom, and, for the most part, everyone was pretty good about cleaning up after themselves.

One day, I was on my way out of my rooms. I grabbed the door and pulled it behind me as I left. The door violently jerked me back into the room. So I pulled again. Same thing — it resisted. It felt like someone was holding it from the other side. This was crazy. After a few more attempts, it finally closed.

The second time this happened, I got my tools and removed the door from its hinges. Nothing was wrong. This was an old wooden door, a lightweight interior door. There was absolutely no reason that this damn door should pull me back into the room, and I was baffled.

At work, my immediate supervisor was something of an historian around Boulder. So, one day, in pleasant conversation, I mentioned the story about the door. You must realize that I had to be discreet in these matters. I worked in the heavy-equipment industry, and stories of this nature would get you a ribbing that would last for months.

I carefully approached the subject, and he didn't hesitate one moment. He said that The Marine House was one of the oldest buildings in town. He then went into his office and brought out an old black-and-white photograph of Boulder. Sure enough, there it was: My temporary residence standing alone in what appeared to be an open field. When I told him about the door, he was not surprised in the least and went on to say that there was a violent history to this particular building stemming from the Gold Rush days. He said a lot of '49ers had met their Maker in this house. There were tales that, at one time or another, there had been a literal bloodbath in the place.

Armed with this information, I quietly went about my business and immediately started looking for another residence.

The Cold Spot

The property in Australia that I rented was old, even by their standards. It was a wooden structure with four bedrooms, a living room, kitchen, and bath, with the "Dunny House" located just outside the door in the back. At some time, they had closed in the back porch with all windows.

This made a terrific studio. I looked out over a wooded valley with tall eucalyptus trees and other Australian flora. The rear of my house was above the slope of the valley so that the entire back of the house looked out over a stand of trees, practically at treetop level. That was where the living room, a spare bedroom, and my studio area were located. So, I had to walk through the living room and into a spare bedroom to access my studio.

Even though I lived in this house and maintained all of the rooms, I had never noticed anything strange — except for the story I'm about to relate.

In Australia at that time, whenever friends came by and you were serving alcohol, it was just accepted that they would spend the evening. The drunk-driving laws were so stiff, no one wanted to risk a run-in with the local Gendarmes.

I had two decent friends there. One was David, who worked for the Fosters Brewery. He was in charge of a shipping department and went to work in a shirt and tie. Neville, my other friend, was the guy who asked me to work at the funeral parlor. He was originally from Sydney, and, whenever the two met, they would always be trading barbs about which city was better. Both had girlfriends toward the middle part of my stay.

One night, l had Neville up to the mountains for a dinner party. At that time, my second wife was living with me, and we made a handsome foursome. We ate a nice meal and drank a lot of wine and other libations into the wee hours. They slept in the spare bedroom near my studio.

During the night, at around 3:00 a.m., Neville woke me up and asked for a blanket. He said that they were freezing in that room. This struck me as being a little odd. The Australian Summer is a hot one. I had seen temperatures of at least 90 degrees during the dead of night. It was hard to sleep with just a sheet — let alone a blanket. I gave them a few blankets, and we all went back to sleep without much more thought on the subject.

Some time passed, though it was still summer, and I invited my friend David up for dinner and drinks. He brought his fiancée, and we had another great meal, with copious amounts of drinking, during and afterward.

Again, they, too, slept in the spare bedroom — and the same thing happened.

About 4:00 a.m., David woke me up and asked for a blanket. He said that he and his girlfriend were cold in that room. I checked the thermometer on the porch — it was 93 degrees.

Without causing any alarm, I just gave them the blankets and waited until they'd left before investigating this occurrence. Sure enough, when I stood in the corner of this bedroom, the temperature dropped by more than 10 degrees. There wasn't any logical explanation. The room was in that portion of the house that stuck out over the hillside. There was nothing beneath it but air.

I obviously had an authentic "cold spot."

My old neighbor had alluded to the fact that this place had a history, but, at the time, he hadn't gone into any detail.

Now I know what he may have been referring
to.

The Ultimate Ghost Story

My late father-in-law, John Fee, started research on his family's origin in Ireland. He spent years compiling data relating to his relatives — I should say "ancestors" — until his labor hit a wall of apathy on the part of officials in Ireland. There is a lack of real records due to a massive fire in Dublin, or so they say. What was needed was on-the-ground detective work. He made one trip to the old sod, but this wasn't quite sufficient in scope to accomplish anything substantial. It would require the diligence and hard work of my wife, Teresa, to fill in the blanks of the Fee family history in Ireland.

Teresa picked up the banner from her father after he passed away in 1995. Prior to this, we had made several trips to Ireland and actually lived in Killarney for four months. But this was before she started delving into her father's research. After John's passing, Teresa's investigation turned serious. It entailed dragging me around the countryside, traipsing through every cemetery that we came upon. For many years, my shoes were perpetually wet, and I assumed the bent-over posture characteristic of a grave robber — with soiled derby, muddy boots, and the telltale lantern, searching tombstones for a magic name.

For a comprehensive understanding, read IRELAND'S MAGDALEN, by Teresa Marie Fee.

We spend between four and six months in Ireland every year. Our home base is the small, sleepy little town of Westport, on the West coast, where Croagh Patrick is located. This is a very distinctive mountain (actually, it is an extinct volcano) overlooking Clew Bay on the West coast of Ireland. There is a rough path going up one side that pilgrims traverse every year as atonement for sins, real and imagined. Consquently, every year, they lift about a dozen of these zealots off the slope via helicopter due to heart attacks, broken bones, and sundry other injuries.

From there, we make journeys into the various areas both North and South of that location. Our landlord leaves a car in our driveway that we can use whenever we care to. It has proven to be a nice, compact arrangement.

Our travels had taken us to the small city of Ballina. We stayed at a B&B just North of the town. As with most B&B stays, you get to chat with the owners and sometimes become lifelong friends. After a brilliant Irish breakfast (the Irish eat a very substantial breakfast — not at all like the British), we were sitting in the parlor, just talking, when my wife started telling our host about her family research. She asked us to step outside, where we could see across the bay that this house was located on, and she proceeded to point across the water and said, "I believe what you are looking for may be right over there."

When we left, we drove South a few miles, around the end of the bay, and then North to about the location that our host had pointed out. There was an old church there, up on a small hill, and we went about looking at various tombstones for the elusive name, "Fee."

On our way to this church, I'd driven through a small valley with one of those five-foot ground fogs in it and thought nothing of it until we were above this place on the hill. Every now and then, the fog would part, and I would catch a glimpse of a structure down in this valley. Finally, I told Teresa that what we were looking for was probably down there, in that depression.

So, we drove down and parked right in front of some rusted iron gates. Naturally, the gates were rusted shut, and I had to use all of my strength to pry it open.

When it finally gave way, it let out this horrible *Screech!* like out of the movies. This was a very old cemetery. All of the tombstones and markers were cantilevered in different directions, and the chapel was all stove in, with a tree growing up through it.

During this time, the fog just seemed to cloak us in a cold and damp garment. The entire scene was what you would expect from a good horror movie.

As we both looked, I heard Teresa announce that she had found it — the real "Fee" tombstone!

They were all there — her father's long-lost ancestors. So she photographed and did a rubbing of the information, and we were done.

25 years of searching came to an abrupt and successful end.

We were both freezing by this time, so I suggested that we go to the car and get warm.

My car on that trip was a brand-new Audi. It was a rental, and it had a nice stereo system in it, which was unusual at that time, because, normally, they'd be missing from the dashboard, due to theft. This stereo had a little red screen with red LED lights and letters. When a song came on, the screen would spell out the name of the artist and the song.

Another item of interest is the significance of the numbers "11/11." That number was not only John Fee's birthdate, but it was also the date he'd returned from Europe after fighting in World War Two. Let's just say that "11/11" held a great deal of significance for the Fee girls.

We sat in the car, trying to decide what to do. Finally, a joint decision was reached to just leave and continue our journey. She had found what she'd been looking for, and she felt relieved.

As soon as I turned the key to start the car, the panel on the dashboard flashed the numbers "11/11" in red LED light, followed by the word "FEE."

These two displays flashed like this for about six seconds while both Teresa and I watched: "11/11" and then "FEE."

I am convinced that John Fee had spoken to us from the beyond. We had accomplished what he did not have the time to finish.

Think about it: There was absolutely no reason that those two things should have been on the dashboard radio display of a rented Audi automobile.

l have never been able to formulate a logical explanation for this set of circumstances.

Epilogue

My childhood was in — and of — another era.

Television was only in black-and-white and the time spent in front of it restricted. My father generally decided what we would watch, and, back then, there wasn't a very wide selection in the first place. We could only receive three channels successfully, and I spent much of my time trying to improve the reception of the elusive "22," the third channel.

It was a case of the grass being greener on that particular channel. They always seemed to have the better programs. At one point, I had an antenna hanging from the old apple tree in our side yard, but, every time the wind would blow, the picture quality would soon follow suit.

My exposure to and my development of a sense of humor derived from early television personalities like Sid Caesar, Ernie Kovacs, Steve Allen, and, of course, the one and only Groucho

Marx. The only place we were allowed to see The Three Stooges was at the Saturday movie-theatre matinee. "The Lark" theatre ran a matinee that included a cliffhanger western and one episode of The Three Stooges. They also gave out door prizes, but, for the life of me, I can't remember what that program was all about. Probably — because I never won anything — I just ignored it.

There wasn't a lot of humor in life back then. In fact, life was just downright nasty and hard. My father was a coalminer. He'd come home from the mines with a really bad attitude. He preferred to kick our asses over sitting around and belly-laughing with his indentured sons. But laughter would and did prevail. We found simple things to laugh about.

As I mentioned in my dedication, all of life is a stage of sorts, and we decide who the real comedians are on the playbill.

These stories comprise particles from that life, starting on the dusty streets of Wilkes-Barre and continuing on to many far-flung places around the world. I have been fortunate that humor has always stayed with me throughout life.

After my combat service in Vietnam, there were times that I would doubt if I would find anything funny about mankind ever again.

There is nothing funny about war, and I wish that mankind as a whole could just realize that and do away with the entire concept.

But, in reality, that is never going to happen — at least not in my lifetime.

I sincerely hope that you have enjoyed these stories. I realize that a few of them might have teetered on the brink of bad taste. At least, that's what my wife said. But I decided to keep even those in the book for the sake of diversity. I realize also that a few of the stories stretch the definition of humor, though it is in there somewhere. These have been observations from my life that have run the full gamut of experience.

We have to laugh — from time to time — especially at ourselves. Without that small outlet for emotion, where would we be? Just simple vessels, empty containers walking through an individual experience, and emerging at the other end with nothing to show for our efforts.

Allow me to congratulate you for being a part of the *Urban Gothic*.

— JG

Made in the USA
Columbia, SC
09 October 2020

22358525R00200